Man's Imprint on Cheshire

By Oliver Bott and Rhys Williams

with a Foreword by The Earl Grosvenor

Oliver Bott MA Cantab, Dip TP Manc, RIBA, MRTPI, is
Conservation Officer and Rhys Williams MA (Archaeology),
Liverpool, RIBA, Fellow of Liverpool University, is
Principal Archaeologist in the Cheshire County Planning
Department.

Published by Cheshire County Council

ISBN 0904532 011

Here is a book to focus our attention and stimulate our interest in the imprint of past and present on the continuing history of our County. For the visitor it will provide a guide to places of interest, for the student of the past a unique reference to the making and the meaning of the rich historic tapestry of Cheshire's varied towns, villages and landscape — and it will help those who must plan for the future to assess what deserves to be conserved or enhanced and what is at risk in our changing scene.

What is of most value or interest in towns and countryside, and how has man co-operated with nature to evolve the beauty and variety of scene?

Leafing through the pages of this book, I find that two themes stand out — the extent to which individual men endowed with special genius or vigour of mind have moulded the development of the County — and the wide variety of talents and skills which have contributed to the quality of our surroundings, and indeed our whole way of life, from pre-Roman times to the present day.

We are thankful for what they have done — and are mindful that the social changes which mark period from period are still at work. One wonders how we today can muster the skills and vigour — and the incentive — not just to conserve the best from the past, but to create the best for the future.

Grosvenor.

Eaton Hall
October 1975

*The Iron Bridge over the Dee to Eaton Park,
Aldford, 1824, by Thomas Telford.*

Contents

Almost the whole surface of lowland Britain bears the marks of man's long occupation and of the changes in his way of life and pattern of settlement which have taken place since prehistoric times. The evidence, above and below ground, can cast light on many aspects of past life — and of death; habitation, agriculture, industry, handiwork and arts, recreation, trade, travel and transport, worship, burial and commemoration.

Man's imprint on the landscape.

No written records of Britain survive from before the Roman period. Some oral legends may give clues to the nature of earlier cultures, but the main and most reliable evidence must come from the fragmentary physical remains which can be identified and interpreted by the archaeologist. Important though writings have been as sources for history since the Roman invasion, records and documents were, until quite recently, laborious to produce and so were generally limited to matters of direct use or interest to the writers or their masters. Consequently, facets of past life and work which would be of great interest to us were taken for granted and so not recorded at the time, and we must rely on archaeological work to provide information.

Documentary and archaeological evidence.

Archaeological records, the local history of architecture and building and the political, economic and social history of a county tend to be treated as different subjects, or at least in different publications. Without attempting to break new ground, this brief review summarises some of the main historical trends and events and relates them to the legacy which former generations have left us in the farmed landscape, towns and villages, communications networks and remains now buried below the ground.

The face of Cheshire and its history.

The Individuality of Cheshire

Conrad made one of his characters say "Man makes history, but history is not made by man. History is made by the force of economic circumstance". Geography, geology and climate lie behind the economic circumstances which give each county — and different parts of each county — their individuality.

Geography, geology and climate.

Cheshire occupies the Midland Gap, the low-lying plain between the Pennines and the North Welsh uplands, and in the north it embraces both banks of the Mersey at Halton and Warrington. This has made it a main corridor of communication since prehistoric times for journeys between the south and the north-west of England and between England and the North Welsh Coast and the ports for Ireland — an important trade link in peacetime and a line of communication in war. Remains from most periods reflect this characteristic.

The glaciers which formed during the last Ice Age on the adjoining uplands flowed down across the Cheshire Plain scouring away any traces of previous settlement and covering the land with a thick glacial drift of heavy clays and sand. Thus nothing has been found or is likely to be found from the Old Stone Age. The action of the glaciers has also affected the subsequent pattern of settlement and life. The predominance of clay soils has suited the land better for pasture than the plough and has helped to secure Cheshire's pre-eminence in dairy farming.

The salt-beds of the Weaver valley, important commerically in their own right at least since Roman days, were also a vital resource for the development of central north Cheshire as the cradle of our modern heavy chemical industry during the 19th century. The presence of coal nearby in the South Lancashire coalfield was also important, as was the limestone brought by rail from Derbyshire.

Salt.

4

Textile mills.

The foothills of the Pennines in East Cheshire had swift-flowing brooks to power the textile mills' water-wheels of the early industrial revolution, but the 18th century water mills of Cheshire were to be overshadowed during the 19th century by the explosive growth of the Lancashire cotton towns where a major coalfield could provide fuel for steam-powered mills. Indeed, the shift of activity to the towns on and around the south Lancashire coalfield may account for the fact that Cheshire has no really large industrial towns. Stockport on the southern fringe of the Manchester conurbation and Birkenhead/Wallasey on the Mersey estuary were the largest before the revision of the County boundary excluded them in 1974, but brought in Warrington, which is now the largest town, mainly standing on the north side of the Mersey.

Building materials; timber and thatch.

Geology and climate affect building methods and materials as well as the pattern of towns and villages, agriculture and industry. The land form and soil of the low-lying plain encouraged the growth of forests with plentiful oak trees, and the level valley-bottoms of the slow-flowing rivers contained extensive marshy reedbeds. So oak frames and daub-and-wattle panels for the walls and reed thatch for the roofs were the materials for most buildings in much of Cheshire at least until the 17th century.

Sandstone.

Sandstone outcrops fairly frequently on the central Cheshire ridge and in other undulating areas of the plain. It is soft, however, and not very durable as a building stone. It requires periodic repair and refacing if it is to survive. It seems to have been little used before the 17th century except for churches and monastic buildings, castles and bridges. The churches and bridges generally remain in use and have been kept in repair, at least to some degree, but their maintenance is expensive. Most of the castle and monastic buildings, long out of use, have suffered severe deterioration. The remains of the West Tower of St. John the Baptist Church in Chester shows how seriously the stonework has decayed since 1881, when its upper storeys fell.

Gritstone.

East Cheshire overlaps the gritstone area of the Peak District. The gritstone is much more durable than the red sandstone of the plain, and is the common walling material of the villages, farms and cottages of the Pennines and their foothills, and of the little cotton-milling town of Bollington. Gritstone slabs are the usual roofing material in the same part of Cheshire, graded in size from the smallest stones at the ridge to the largest at the eaves.

Brick, tiles and slates.

The clay beds which the glaciers of the last ice age deposited on the plain provide material for brick-making, but apparently they were little exploited until the 17th century. From that time, however, bricks were produced and used increasingly, and began to supersede timber framing as the predominant walling material. (Indeed, they began to be used to replace even the wattle-and-plaster panels between the posts and struts of the old oak-framed buildings). By the 18th century brick was the norm in central and west Cheshire, although local stone was commonly used for every-day building work when it could be found close at hand.

Lumbhole Mill, Kettleshulme, in a Pennine Valley.

The White Lion, Barthomley, 1614.

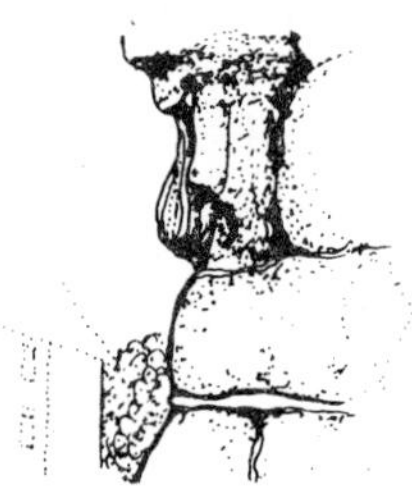

Weathered soft Cheshire sandstone. St John the Baptist Church, Chester.

A Pennine Cottage, Sutton Lane Ends, Macclesfield.

Frodsham Main Street, late 18th century doorway.

View near Timbersbrook, Congleton — trees help to make a fine landscape.

Grey slates (sometimes blue-grey and sometimes purplish) became common in most of Cheshire during the 18th century, as improved inland transport brought them in to compete with the local thatch. The city of Chester was to some extent a precursor; with ready access to the North Welsh coast by sea, slates were used there even in the Middle Ages. The making of tiles seems to have followed on closely from the making of bricks. Generally hard-burned dark blue-grey, but sometimes dark red or brown, their use spread from the south-east concurrently with the use of slate from Wales.

Main Themes and Problems

These are the themes which recur in the following chapters: Cheshire as a main corridor of communications in peace and war — prehistoric tracks, Roman roads, the Marches and the shipping of the Middle Ages, 18th century canals and turnpike roads, Victorian railways and shipping navigations, and modern motorways; the slow development of the pastoral landscape of the countryside; the long history of salt extraction in the Weaver Valley and the growth from it of the heavy chemical industry; the 18th century textile industries of the Pennine foothills; the changes over the centuries in society, economy and technology and in the roles of the towns and some of the villages; the development of building materials and techniques and the broadening range of purposes which buildings have served. The themes raise the questions: What are the most serious gaps in our knowledge of past settlement and life in Cheshire and what can we do to lessen them? What parts of our legacy from the past do we value most? — What should we record before it is destroyed and what should we seek to protect from destruction? Are there serious gaps in the protection which the law provides for our heritage or in the aid which it allows from public funds? Does our tax system threaten the survival of well-maintained landed estates or of some of the most interesting and valuable of our larger buildings? What specific threats do current developments pose — for instance, new building, sand working and quarrying, traffic, new roads and road improvements, pipelines, changes in farming methods?

What action is needed, what should be done first and what can we afford? Decisions made now could affect the interest and attractiveness of the face of Cheshire well into the 21st century.

Pre-Roman Cheshire

The Earlier Stone Ages

Glaciers of the last Ice Age.

There are no remains in Cheshire of the greater part of man's long prehistory. The Ice Ages brought arctic conditions to Britain; the ice caps came as far south as the Midlands and the slow movement of glaciers from the Pennines and the Welsh mountains scoured away any evidence which there may have been of earlier man from the plain between.

With the last retreat of ice some ten thousand years ago, man returned. As the ice melted, the land which had been beneath it lifted, but so did the sea level, and Britain (formerly joined to the Continent with a low-lying isthmus), became an island. The arctic climate slowly became sub-arctic and then temperate. What had been tundra became woodland, and with the change of conditions came a change of economy. Men were still hunters and food gatherers rather than farmers, but progressively relying on fishing and the capture of small animals and birds rather than the bigger game. This is clearly seen in the tools of the Mesolithic or middle stone-using period. They are much smaller than those of the earlier Palaeolithic or old stone-using period and much more specialised. Small flint arrowheads, of a type used to bring down birds and small animals with a minimum of damage to plumage and pelt, are evidence of skill with the bow. Other tools were composite, and one such tool, a sickle composed of several small sharp flints set in a bone or wooden handle, shows that wild corn was being reaped.

The distribution of stone weapons and tools

Flint tools are popularly associated with the chalk lands of the south. They are, however, common elsewhere and quantities of tools made of flint or chert (a flint-like stone) have been found on the higher, drier ground and sandy places in North-West England and North Wales. Any well-drained, lightly wooded area, with reasonable access to fresh water, or low sandy coastal land with its potential for good fishing and water transport, is likely to produce evidence of human activity from this time. Amongst such places in Cheshire that have yielded flints of Mesolithic type are Alderley Edge and Frodsham — and New Ferry and Meols in the Wirral peninsular which is now in the Merseyside County. Either the tools or the flint from which to make them had to be imported from flint-bearing land.

Settlements in the Middle Stone Age (c. 10,000 B.C. to c. 3,500 B.C.). Indirect evidence.

Unlike the preceding Palaeolithic period, more and more occupation sites of Mesolithic times are being found. These include flint-working floors, hearths and even simple houses, usually sunk a little below ground level. Houses have not, as yet, been found in Cheshire but finds such as those from Frodsham, with concentrations over a wide area of waste flakes, finished tools and the shaped cores of good quality flint from which they were struck, must surely indicate a nearby habitation of some kind. Other sites in Cheshire, dating from the end of this period, bear witness to trade and to travel. For example, flint tools of a distinctive Irish type have been found at Meols and New Ferry. They could only have reached Britain by boat over the Irish Sea, although it is unlikely that the crossing was made direct to the Wirral coast at that time; it would involve too long a sea voyage.

The Neolithic Period (c. 3,500 B.C. to c. 1,800 B.C.)

Neolithic tools — trade and distribution.

Communication and trade are even more in evidence in the next phase of pre-history in Cheshire. This is the Neolithic or New Stone Age, differentiated because many of the tools found, unlike those of earlier periods, were ground smooth after being chipped to shape — especially the small stone axes which seem to be the characteristic tools of the period.

The significance of these stone axes is far greater than the mere fact that they were ground smooth. Whilst some were made of flint, a great many of them were of fine-grained volcanic rocks not found in Cheshire or elsewhere in lowland England. Amongst the axes found in Cheshire are those of stone from Langdale Pike in Cumbria and Penmaenmawr in North Wales. At both places, axe factories have been discovered where rough-outs were produced to be traded all over Britain. The distribution of these axes in the Wirral and along the Weaver and some of the other rivers probably indicates well defined lines of communication which were the routes of trade within the county.

Flint burin or graving tool.

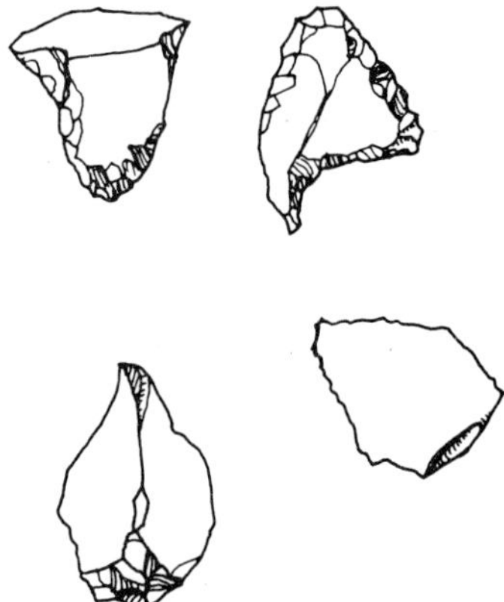

Middle Stone Age arrow and lance heads.

Polished stone axe-head.

The other great significance of the Neolithic axe is that it was an agricultural tool used in a "slash and burn" type of agriculture; trees were felled and burned and crops grown in the clearings.

Agriculture is now considered to be amongst the main characteristics of the Neolithic period, at least in Britain. The first agriculturalists arrived here some 5,000 to 5,500 years ago. However, hunting still played its part in community life, and distinctive arrowheads of the period are found in Cheshire. It is interesting to see evidence in some of these of the fusion of the traditions of the new farmers with those of the earlier Mesolithic hunters. Arrowheads of these mixed cultures are to be found in Cheshire.

Crop growing and stock raising usually meant settlement but no actual habitation sites of the period have, so far, been identified in Cheshire. As in the preceding phase, the well-drained, lightly wooded land was most likely to be settled and any such areas in Cheshire may reveal archaeological remains from the period. The manufacture of pottery is a further main characteristic of this period.

Settlement, no less than a nomadic hunting life, was associated with organised religion and belief in an afterlife. There is one clearly identified communal burial chamber of the Neolithic period in Cheshire. This is the Bridestones, near Congleton, which is a court cairn. The name is given to a type of tomb in front of which there is a court defined by large stone uprights. The type occurs on both sides of the northern part of the Irish Sea.

One period merges into another and before the end of the true stone-using Neolithic Age, bronze weapons and other objects were being introduced into Britain. This was in the so-called Beaker period, when there was a widespread movement throughout Europe of people using a distinctive type of pottery beaker.

The Bronze Age (c. 1,800 B.C. to c. 500 B.C.)

This term broadly means that period when bronze had generally supplanted the use of stone, wood and bone for many edged and pointed tools and for personal ornaments etc. It is generally held to refer to a period lasting from c. 1,800 — c. 500 B.C.

Flint was not wholly abandoned at this time and was still commonly used for small edged and pointed tools. Examples of all these objects are found in Cheshire. Technologically, however, the period was a great advance over the preceding one. The casting of bronze developed from simple flat shapes to the complicated hollow-cast bronzes using the cire perdue, or "lost wax core" process. A model of the object was made in wax which, in turn, was covered with clay. When this was baked, the wax ran out leaving a hollow clay mould in which the object could be cast in bronze. Much of the work was evidently carried out by itinerant bronze smiths whose stocks of scrap bronzes are sometimes found. The spearheads, bronze rods and the socketted axe found at Congleton are part of just such a hoard. (It is, perhaps, as well for historians that our ancestors were not as litter conscious as we are today!)

The trackways and the barrows or circular Bronze Age burial mounds which can still be seen, particularly in the Macclesfield and Peak Park areas, show that there was considerable movement about the County. A trail of sites and stray finds indicate a similar route along the Mersey, at least westward from Warrington. A line of burial mounds and stray finds from Appleton and Grappenhall to Winwick and Golborne suggests that Warrington may also have been important as a crossing place of the Mersey. Another route from the Mersey starts at Helsby and Frodsham and runs southward along the sandstone ridge to Beeston and beyond; the number of barrows at Utkinton on this route suggest a settlement there.

The barrows, which often contain more than one interment, are evidence just as much for settlement as for people passing through. Barrows are to be found, here and there, throughout Cheshire, on high ground and on the sand and gravel subsoils. Many have already been destroyed but some are protected as Ancient Monuments and others no doubt still remain to be recognised for what they are.

The Bridestones near Congleton — upright stones from a court cairn, burial chamber on right.

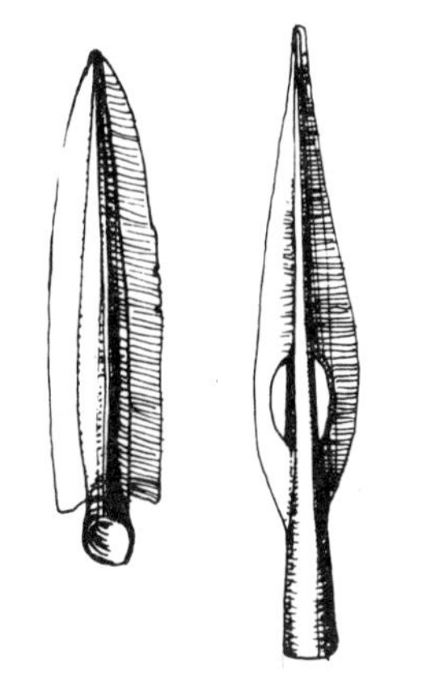

Bronze spearheads from Congleton.

Burial mound near Macclesfield.

It used to be assumed that Cheshire was almost unpopulated even in late pre-historic times, largely because no great evidence had been found to suggest otherwise. However, a careful perusal of aerial photographs is now gradually revealing (by shadows cast by low sun or early ripening marks in fields of corn) a number of features which could be unrecorded pre-historic sites.

Similarly, a series of finds of related features and objects suggest there may have been a Bronze Age settlement at Grappenhall. It is also now known from the Midland counties, notably Northamptonshire, that heavy glacial clay lands began to be settled at this time rather than much later as was formerly thought. This could well apply to Cheshire.

There is evidence in the Delamere area of "Celtic fields". These are groups of small square prehistoric fields, bounded by earth banks (lynchets), almost ploughed out. The fields are usually associated with at least one homestead. There are also suggestions of linear banks, here and there, possibly the remnants of ranch boundaries which, although often of the Bronze Age, are of later date than the Celtic fields.

Neolithic and Bronze Age society — place names.

It is now thought that an advanced tribal society, based on blood relationship and including the concept of kingship, had developed during the Neolithic period and had become well established in Britain during the Bronze Age. This is in keeping with what is known of Celtic society and it is generally agreed that the people of that Age were Celtic speaking. It is possible, therefore, that many of the place-names of Celtic origin in eastern and central Cheshire date from as far back as c. 1,800 to c. 500 B.C., particularly the names of natural features such as rivers, for example Gowy, Weaver, Wheelock and Dane.

Socketted bronze axe from Congleton.

The Early Iron Age (from c. 500 B.C. onwards)

The Hallstatt and La Tène cultures.

The first use of iron in this country was as late as c. 500 B.C. when it was introduced as part of the Hallstatt culture (named after the place where it was first defined) which spread outwards from Central Europe. This early phase is characterised by certain pottery types, shapes of sword blades etc.

The succeeding La Tène phase (also named after a place) is probably better known for the often spectacular examples of the rich, swirling ornamental patterns of Celtic art, the chariot burials of Yorkshire, and the well-publicised lake villages of Glastonbury and Meare (examples of which may also occur in Cheshire; this is yet to be investigated).

The last phase of all was that of the great British kingdoms of the South-East, such as that of Cunobelinus (Shakespeare's Cymebline), with their native gold coinage and import of rich goods from the Roman world beyond the Channel.

Gold torque or neck ornament.

There is little evidence that these flowerings of the Celtic culture had much impact on Cheshire and the surrounding counties. The new iron-using peoples were of the same Celtic-speaking stock as those already here, and doubtless had the same organisations and customs. No real difference is therefore to be expected, perhaps, beyond the gradual introduction of iron, in those areas some distance away from the European mainland.

Hill forts — evidence of unrest.

However, the Early Iron Age must have been a period of considerable unrest and Cheshire, like the neighbouring counties to the north, south and west, had its quota of hillforts. As was the case elsewhere, these were enlarged and strengthened at least once during their lifetime.

The Cheshire forts are in two groups of three, with one standing alone. The groups are Helsby Hill, Woodhouses Hill and Bradley in the north; Eddisbury, Kelsborrow Castle (Kelsall) and the Oakmere earthwork in the centre; with the one fort at Maiden Castle (Bickerton) in the south. The Eddisbury hill-fort was particularly impressive, with an inturned entrance defended by a stout gate, the postholes for which were found during excavations. It also contained a number of rather small circular dwellings of the period.

Maiden Castle, Bickerton.

A defended homestead.

The central sandstone ridge on which the hillforts are located runs from Helsby and Frodsham in the north via Delamere to the Beeston Gap and from thence southwards to the Malpas area where it is of a more broken nature. It appears to have been a major route of prehistoric travel.

Iron Age routes.

As with the preceding periods, no definite Early Iron Age settlement or homestead has been found in Cheshire, although they must have existed, judging from indirect evidence. In the rest of Britain and Ireland homesteads of the period were elaborate round houses of 45-60 feet across, usually with attendant farms, enclosures and field systems. They are rarely distinguishable, without excavation, from their Bronze Age counterparts except, perhaps, by size.

Settlements and homesteads.

Not all Iron Age structures were round as was once supposed, and more and more examples of rectangular dwellings are being found. In some areas, these seem to have been built in bays — a system using heavy principal frames and roof trusses previously thought not to have been developed until the Middle Ages.

The Early Iron Age folk culture in Cheshire gradually merged into the Roman, or more correctly the Romano-British, culture. The Roman settlements at Chester, Northwich, Middlewich and Wilderspool no doubt had citizens Romanised to a greater or lesser degree. No doubt, too, the farming Briton of the Cheshire countryside remained in culture a Celt, for there was a widespread resurgence of the native tongue and native customs after the withdrawal of the Legions from Britain, about A.D. 410.

Folk culture.

It may be, therefore, that there was a continuing and underlying folk tradition in Cheshire and the neighbouring counties which ranged in time from the Bronze Age right through into the Dark Ages and perhaps beyond.

Comment

The period from the end of the last Ice Age to the coming of the Romans represents four fifths of the time during which man is known to have occupied the land which is now Cheshire. This is a county where archaeologists have, until recently, been much less active than in the chalklands of southern England. The development of our knowledge of pre-history in Britain and Ireland as a whole suggests that settlement and culture in Cheshire were sufficiently significant and firmly established to deserve more vigorous investigation. Successive changes in the pattern of settlement and land use from Roman times to the present day have obscured or destroyed much which the people of the Stone, Bronze and Iron ages had left. The recording or preservation of such remaining pieces of the jigsaw as are known or can be found is vital if we are to reconstruct any coherent picture of so distant a past.

Some of the most significant among these remaining pieces may well be found in or near one of Cheshire's peat mosses, such as those in Delamere and Oakmere or near Congleton, Macclesfield and Alsager. Peat deposits can be dated within broad limits and, with their plant remains and rich pollen content, they give a clear indication of the climate and natural environment which existed when they were formed. It follows that any evidence of human activity, such as man-made objects or the remains of structures found in the peat can be dated with it and be related to a particular past natural environment. This is especially important for an understanding of the beginning of early settled life in Britain. Already the dating of the earliest farming communities of the Neolithic period, or New Stone Age, has been pushed back by over a thousand years in Britain to about 3,500 B.C. Hardly any work has been done in this field of research in the North-West and none at all in Cheshire: nothing is really known of our earliest communities. A study of the relationship between finds and their original botanical context could give some unexpected results. Such a study would be a fascinating as well as an important one.

A thousand years of invasions — The Roman Conquest to the Norman Conquest

The Romans in Cheshire

Drive and competence.

The Romans in Britain were conquerors, organisers and engineers; builders in massive stonework; writers of factual reports and records — the first civilisation in north-western Europe to provide us with coherent documentary evidence of their life and works. But they were also propagandists; they wrote of their own achievements rather than of the life and culture of the peoples whom they conquered. The durability of their structures and the survival of their writings have left substantial remains and a good key with which to interpret them. The complexity and sophistication of their society, occupations, industry and administration mean that they produced as wide a variety of buildings and artefacts in this part of Britain as any succeeding age until the 16th or 17th century.

The military importance of Deva (Chester).

The Romans conquered Britain from the south. They never fully penetrated the mountains of Scotland, Wales and northern England with their civilian culture, and the low-lying land adjoining the mountains, including Cheshire, remained largely a military zone. Chester was the pivot of their three permanent legionary fortresses, Isca (Caerleon), Deva and Eboracum. The XXth Legion at Deva had to be fed, housed and equipped. Soldiers wholly occupied the fortress within the Roman walls, and they controlled the production of essential materials in industrial settlements nearby — Holt (in Clwyd) where tiles and pottery were made, and possibly Heronbridge.

Outside the walls of Deva was the vicus or civilian trading settlement which depended on the fortress for business and protection. This is thought to have centred on Foregate Street. On the other side of the fortress was the port. The quays were on the Roodee, which the estuary then partly covered.

Communications.

Efficient transport was essential to the Romans' success. Deva, like all their main military bases, had to be a focus of communication. It needed the port for seaward traffic as well as good roads to link with the other fortresses, administrative, industrial and commercial centres. A network of Roman roads criss-crosses the Cheshire plain with the most important routes leading to Chester.

One of the best examples of the typical direct Roman Road is the A530 from Broken Cross, Northwich, south in a dead straight line for 3 miles towards Middlewich. Over this length the modern road probably coincides with the line of the Roman "King" Street. The Cheshire Plain emerged under the Romans for the first time as a nationally important corridor of communications serving a unified administration.

Civilian towns — industry.

There were subsidiary forts and camps elsewhere in Cheshire, but Wilderspool, Condate (Northwich) and Salinae (Middlewich) appear to have been substantial civilian settlements during much of the Roman period. Northwich and Middlewich lived mainly by the production of salt but Wilderspool shows evidence of a wider variety of industry. There may also have been a salt producing settlement at Nantwich.

Apart from the remains of buildings and roads in and between these towns, as in Deva, the distribution of coins and inscribed tablets gives important evidence of the period during which settlements were occupied, and some clue as to the points in time when they were most active.

The British under the Romans — domestic life and agriculture.

The British Celts inhabited the civilian settlements. The Cornovii were the tribe who occupied land which is now Cheshire and part of Shropshire and Staffordshire. Excavation has revealed a good deal about the nature and equipment of their industries but very little of their society or domestic life. Even less is known of the countryside. Some of the land must have been farmed actively to produce sufficient crops and herds to feed the legionaries and the townspeople, but no evidence has been found of the Roman type of agricultural villa in Cheshire. The old Celtic methods of farming seem to have endured throughout the Roman period, but no traces have yet been identified of the distribution of rural settlements, buildings, or field patterns which can be ascribed to that time.

Amphitheatre, Chester — entrance to arena.

The degree to which the written records and the identified remains in Cheshire cast light on the Roman conquest, administration and communications rather than on the civilian life and society of the conquered Britons may make it tempting to concentrate further investigation on what is already best known or most easily ascertained. There is a good deal still to be found out about the Romans in Cheshire, but it is likely to clarify details of their buildings, life and organisation rather than to cast a new light on the nature of their rule. At Deva it may also explain more fully the development and vicissitudes of the fortress during the three centuries and more of its life.

Investigation of the Celtic settlements and culture under the Romans deserves more attention than it has yet had, both for the interest of what may be revealed in its own right and as a link in the development of the native society between the Iron Age and the post-Roman Dark Ages. This is, so far, an almost untouched field.

Cheshire in the Dark Ages — from the departure of the Romans to The Norman Conquest

The Roman presence encouraged trade, industry, the mining of ores and the extraction of salt without deeply imposing its imprint on agriculture or civilian life. Their most enduring legacy was the adoption of Christianity and its transmission, when they left, to the Celtic Church. From the 4th to the early 7th century the territory which was later to become Cheshire reverted to the British, but with the Church maintaining a focus of learning. There were many monasteries, but the monks led a simple life and did not usually build in stone, unlike their Norman successors.

The Celtic Church — continuity of culture.

Cheshire stood at the border of the Welsh princedoms of Gwynedd and Powys on the one hand and the North British kingdom of Northumbria (and in the early stages, Strathclyde) and the Saxon kingdom of Mercia on the other. The Wirral peninsular and the Dee estuary were also vulnerable to raids and coastal settlement from the Norse colonies in Ireland. In such a position the shire had an eventful history and absorbed the impact of several cultures.

The frontier of Celtic, Saxon, Irish-Norse and Danish cultures.

The Mercian penetration from the Midlands during the 7th century (first to the Gowy, then the Dee and finally as far as Offa's Dyke to Prestatyn and the Clwydian hills) was largely peaceful, the Saxons and the Welsh often joining to resist the threats of Northumbria.

The Mercian kings who succeeded Offa (757-796) may have lacked his vigour, but the Saxon settlements appear to have remained with little disturbance until the Norsemen from Ireland began to raid and settle in the Wirral and West Cheshire during the second half of the 9th century. So, when Danish rule at last embraced Cheshire early in the 11th century, population and culture had assimilated Celtic, Saxon and Scandinavian elements. The wise Canute made the Saxon Earl Leofric* governor of Mercia, and adopted the laws of the former King Edgar (who had had close links with Chester). During this period Cheshire first emerged as a shire, the major Anglo-Saxon unit of legal administration.

During the whole of the Dark Ages large parts of Cheshire were woodland and marsh which remained uncultivated, but the relatively peaceful Mercian settlement led to the extension of farming to cover most of West Cheshire and North Central Cheshire, and the valleys of the Weaver and Dane. Place names ending in "ham" or "ingham" are common in those areas, and indicate village settlement of Saxon origin.

Agriculture.

The Saxon system of farming with three large open fields tilled co-operatively, dominant in the Midlands, was not fully adopted in Cheshire. The Celtic methods with smaller, squarish fields and small scattered villages or hamlets appear to have survived. The settlement pattern of much of rural Cheshire may still reflect this Celtic influence, especially since the nature of soil and climate, suitable for pasture rather than tillage, did not encourage the larger, compact Anglo-Saxon type of village.

*Whose wife was Lady Godiva

Dark Ages Cross in Chapel, Lyme Park.

12

Of urban settlements, Chester may have been continuously occupied from Roman times, and was to become an important regional centre licensed to mint money from the 9th century onward. As a seaport, stronghold, trading town and monastic centre, Chester in the Dark Ages is of great potential archaeological interest, but few remains have yet been found. A settlement at Warrington is probable, but the clues to this are in its position at the head of the Mersey estuary and the unusual Saxon dedication of its church (St. Elphin) rather than physical remains. Ten dugout canoes were found in Warrington between 1894 and 1941, and it had been thought that these belonged to the Iron Age. However, contractors working at Sankey Bridges in 1971 dug up part of another canoe which has been carbon dated. This indicates that it is between 860 and 1,040 years old, in which case it would date from the later part of the Dark Ages. The canoes which were previously found cannot now be dated, but they are of a similar type — possibly evidence of settlement in the Dark Ages rather than the pre-Roman Iron Age. The salt towns — at least Middlewich and Nantwich — appear to have been occupied and the salt beds exploited.

No Saxon buildings remain in Cheshire. There are a few stone crosses, grave slabs and hoards of small articles such as brooches which reflect Northumbrian, Celtic, Mercian and Irish Norse influence. Coins from the Chester mint date from about 890 A.D.

Physical remains from the Dark Ages.

Buildings and other remains from the Dark Ages are scarce anywhere in England. The Celts, Anglo-Saxons, Norsemen and Danes appear to have built little in stone, and no more than traces of their timber and thatch have survived. The Cheshire Plain was apparently fairly well settled and towards the end of the period Chester was evidently an important and prosperous centre. Nevertheless, following William I's conquest of England, the settlements and farmland of Cheshire suffered wholesale destruction in the reprisals which followed the rebellion in the north-west. This ruthless military action appears to have been aimed at overthrowing Saxon society and what remained of their economy as well as their buildings, and is likely to make it unusually difficult to identify and interpret such traces as may survive in Cheshire from the Dark Ages in the pattern and form of settlements and the cultivation of the land. Perhaps because of its difficulty, the period has been little investigated archaeologically. It is a subject potentially of great interest, but the nature and range of what may be found is uncertain.

St Olave's Church, Lower Bridge Street, Chester — an Irish-Norse dedication, but no remains of the original building.

Remains of Saxon dugout canoe at Warrington Museum.

Cleulow Cross, south-east of Macclesfield (no public access).

Remains from the Roman, Saxon and Medieval Periods

Part of the **Roman walls** at Chester.

Detail of the Saxon Cross at Sandbach.

Norman Chapel, Prestbury. This probably served as the Parish Church in the early Middle Ages.

Doddington Castle, near Nantwich. A small 14th century tower for local defence.

A defensive moat. Motte and bailey castle, Aldford.

Medieval Communications: A pack-horse road near Christleton, Hockenhull Lane.

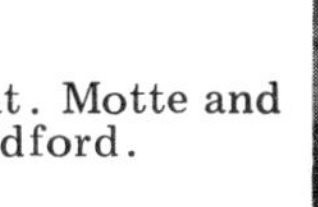

The medieval wall enclosed about twice as much land as the roman wall.

As agricultural prosperity grew during the later Middle Ages the older manor houses were replaced by larger and more comfortable Halls.

Gawsworth Old Hall near Macclesfield. Pre-reformation roof trusses suggest a late medieval origin.

The Old Dee Bridge, Chester. Chester was a major centre for trade and communications and a main military base. The bridge may have had a fortified tower where the larger arch now stands.

Interior of Bunbury Parish Church. Parishes such as Bunbury and Nether Alderley were very large in area during the Middle Ages and each contained a number of townships.

Siddington Church, heavily restored. Oak was the easiest building material to hand on the Cheshire plain. Thus timber framing was used for churches as well as secular buildings.

Nether Alderley Parish Church. Prosperous farming and greater civil wealth in the late 14th, 15th and 16th centuries encouraged the building of large churches.

The Early Middle Ages — 1066 to 1284

During the Middle Ages northern England fared less well than the south, and was lightly populated. Before the Norman conquest Cheshire had enjoyed a period of relative prosperity. Following the conquest and the rebellion against William in the north-west, the Norman army laid waste its countryside, villages and towns (1071). William put the county in charge of Hugh Lupus whom he invested, as Earl of Chester, with almost viceregal powers — a situation which was to continue through a long line of Norman earls. From 1066 until 1284, peace was at best uneasy along the Welsh Border. The Normans, like the Romans, constantly sought to consolidate and extend their rule. Chester regained its importance as a military centre commanding as it does the North Welsh coast and providing the best route by sea to central and northern Ireland. In fact Chester was the largest medieval town in north-west England and the main seaport north of Bristol.

Chester remained at most times a base well behind the zone where the battles and skirmishes took place. The Welsh border fluctuated with the fortunes of war, but generally Cheshire extended to both banks of the Dee and the forward Norman lines embraced the castles of Mold and Hawarden.

Chester owed its importance as a trading town to its seaport, but as a military and administrative centre primarily to its position as the northern hinge of the border with the principalities of Wales, commanding the lowest crossing of the Dee. Behind the town, the Cheshire plain provided the natural corridor of communication for trade and war.

The most substantial remains of the medieval fortifications are Chester's walls and castle founded by William the Conqueror, the later castle on the dramatic sandstone outcrop at Beeston (c.1220) which Randall Blundeville, Earl of Chester, built, apparently to protect his rear against attack by possible rivals from the east, and the baronial castle (partly remodelled in 1800) on the rock at Halton. The string of earth and timber or stone motte-and-bailey castles along the Dee valley — Shotwick, Dodleston, Pulford, Aldford, Castleton, Shocklach and Malpas — are examples of fortifications for local defence. There is a well-preserved 14th century crenellated stone tower at Doddington Park, south-east of Nantwich, sites of Norman castles in central Cheshire at Runcorn, Frodsham, Northwich and Nantwich, and of what was probably a crenellated house rather than a castle at Macclesfield.

The Earls of Chester often had a great need for men-at-arms to protect their earldom or to fight in Wales or in the larger-scale wars in France. Since criminal punishment and even outlawry could sometimes be commuted for military service, Cheshire attracted men who were ready for battle but lawless in peacetime. The motte-and-baileys may have served as much for civil protection within Cheshire as for defence against Welsh raiders.

If Norman Cheshire, like Roman Cheshire, was a military zone, the Normans seem to have done less than the Romans to stimulate trade and industry. The Domesday survey (c.1086) records much "wasted" land (farms devastated in the reprisals of 1071) and no substantial town except Chester. Since Domesday generally enumerates only heads of free households and does not systematically record their families, dependants and bondsmen, it gives an imperfect base for estimating population. From this incomplete evidence it seems that in the 1080's the whole county may have held as few as 2,000 inhabitants, and in any case no more than 1% of its present number.

Agricola Tower, Chester — remains of Norman Castle on Roman foundations.

Outer Gatehouse, Beeston Castle, mid 13th century.

The Rebellion which followed the Norman Conquest brought reprisals which devastated the farmland, depopulated and laid waste the settlements of Saxon Cheshire.

Chester, military base and seaport.

Fortifications.

A martial society.

So small a population deprived of wealth, buildings and equipment by recent war and harassment, cannot have had the resources to recreate prosperity quickly. They were further hampered by the structure and aims of Norman society. The royal or baronial forests occupied much of the Cheshire countryside — Wirral, the two parts of Delamere (Mare and Mondrum stretching from the Mersey to Nantwich) and Macclesfield. The forests were not necessarily woodland, but they were reserved for the hunting of deer and other game by the King, the Earl or their nominees, and so were largely closed to farming. Outside the forests the greatest landholdings were the manors belonging to the Earl, the King, or, increasingly, the monasteries. This left little room for smaller land-owners to get a foothold. Tenants had to provide their lords with their own service and with additional men-at-arms in time of war and, since the need to fight was fairly frequent, farmers and labourers could not give all their energies to farming or improving land and buildings.

Norman domestic architecture is rare anywhere in England. None exists in Cheshire. The only buildings to remain are military or ecclesiastical and one rare example with packhorse bridges, of what appears to have been a medieval road (perhaps the main horse route from Chester to the South and London) at Hockenhull Lane between Christleton and Tarvin.

Parishes and parish churches.

Very little Norman work remains in the parochial churches of Cheshire. The parishes in southern, central and eastern Cheshire were usually very large, each church serving a number of small, scattered villages. The extent of the forests, the continuing Celtic influence on the pattern of rural settlements from before the Norman conquest, the degree to which soil and climate were better suited to pasture than tillage and the concentration of manors in the hands of the Earls of Chester and the monasteries may all have contributed to this and such parish churches as were built were likely to be small and simple, apt to be rebuilt later in the Middle Ages as prosperity grew. Prestbury has the only rural Norman church to remain more or less intact. The much larger present parish church was built two centuries and more later a short distance away, so the original building was allowed to survive.

Monasteries.

Three Norman monasteries in Cheshire were large and splendid. Substantial parts of St. Werburgh's, Chester, have survived because the Benedictine Abbey Church was transformed into a new Cathedral on the dissolution of the monasteries.* The remains of Combermere are for archaeological investigation, little being above ground. Norton Priory is, in 1975, newly excavated. A site of remarkable interest, it displays much information on the development, the plan and organisation of a major priory, with some fine remains of Norman masonry and craftsmanship. Ince provides an interesting and rare example of a monastic grange, a farming community of St. Werburgh's Abbey. At Stanlow Point there are remains of a small and isolated monastic foundation, which was abandoned in the Middle Ages in favour of a new site at Whalley in Lancashire. St. John's at Chester is the only substantially Norman and Transitional (12th — early 13th century) large church to remain in Cheshire. It stands on a Saxon monastic site, and was a collegiate (or quasi monastic) church, and for a short time served as the Cathedral of Lichfield diocese. Although very different from their simple Saxon precedessors, the Norman monastic centres continued to nurture the learning which had survived through the Church's efforts from the last century of the Roman Empire.

Of the towns, Chester stands out for size, importance and the variety of functions which it fulfilled — military base, administrative and judicial centre, the largest port in the North West and, for the north of England, a major centre of trade. However, almost everything within the city walls has been rebuilt at least once since the early Middle Ages.

*Most of the Norman Abbey was rebuilt later in the Middle Ages.

Doorway, St Edith's Church, Shocklach, probably early 12th century.

Medieval boundary wall at Ince — a grange of St Werburgh's Abbey, Chester.

St John the Baptist's Church, Chester — lower stonework Norman, late 12th century above.

Warrington may well have been a relatively important town, but this is a matter for archaeological and historical investigation, for little visible remains from the period. The same is true but on a smaller scale of the salt towns of Nantwich, Middlewich and Northwich, and of Congleton, Macclesfield and the old village of Halton.

The brine springs in the Weaver Valley were no doubt exploited during the Dark Ages, just as they were in Romano-British Cheshire, but documentary and physical evidence leave no doubt that the salt industry flourished during the Middle Ages. The medieval salters used similar methods to the Romans, obtaining brine from the salt springs and evaporating it in lead pans over log fires — a dangerous sounding process; we do not know how much of the lead was eaten, having found its way into the salt. Nantwich appears to have outshone both Middlewich and Northwich as a producer, and to have been a well-established town at least from the 13th century. Although it brought prosperity to the Weaver Valley salt towns and it was a widely traded commodity vital for the preservation of meat for the winter, it does not seem to have affected the economy or pattern of settlements outside the immediate area of its production. The medieval development of the salt towns offer an interesting field for investigation, as recent excavations in Nantwich have confirmed.

Salt.

From unification with Wales to the end of the 14th Century (1284 — 1399)

For Cheshire the most important event of the 13th century was the conquest of Wales and its effective unification under the English crown by Edward I in 1284. Although trade with the Welsh principalities, flourishing before the Norman conquest, continued sporadically during the two centuries which followed it, the border was constantly unsettled. The Norman craving for territory and power had inevitably subordinated civil prosperity to military needs. When peace was finally established the way lay open for the improvement of farming, the growth of trade and the betterment of civil life. Cheshire remained a recruiting ground for men-at-arms for the wars in France and the population retained some reputation for unruliness, but at least there was no local warfare on local English soil.

The sword and the arrow were not the only killers of the young and the strong. Disease was an unpredictable hazard against which there was little effective defence. If the Black Death was the worst single epidemic, carrying away one in four of those living in England in 1348, there were other more local outbreaks which would retard development.

Throughout the thirteenth and fourteenth centuries the monasteries increased their wealth and extended their ownership of land through gifts and legacies — and the Cistercian abbey of Vale Royal, endowed by King Edward I and also associated with later medieval kings and their queens was intended to be the most splendid of English abbeys — to be known as "the Vale Royal of England". Its buildings should have been completed by 1360, but at that time they suffered catastrophic storm damage, and may never have been rebuilt fully as originally planned. Stephen Harding consolidated the Cistercian Order at Citeaux in 1098, and with its simple rule of life it rapidly spread across Western Europe and into Britain. The 12th century saw the finest flowers of our grandly simple early Gothic architecture. When Vale Royal was planned a century later a less austere rule of life seems to have been allowed. The buildings were correspondingly more ornate. Accounts covering the long period of the building works at Vale Royal, unlike the monastery, have survived. They are an invaluable source of information on medieval building. The part which the monasteries played in developing the countryside during this period deserves investigation.

The monasteries.

During the 13th century castles were enlarged and strengthened and (before the final subjugation of Wales) Chester's walls were improved. Conditions favoured domestic building in all the richer parts of Cheshire, but very little has survived. Church building increased, but, except perhaps in Chester, did not reach its peak until the 15th century.

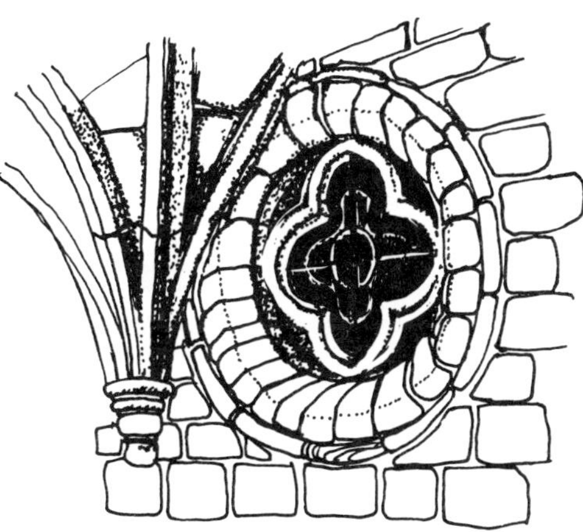

Circular opening, the Cloister, Chester Cathedral, 13th century Early English work.

Saighton Grange Gatehouse — oriel window and doorway, about 1500.

Whether or not there was much general improvement of roads is not known but some major bridges were built; the finest survivors are the Old Dee Bridge at Chester and the Farndon-Holt Bridge (both of which, in the Middle Ages, may have carried defensive towers).

While the 14th century laid the foundation for the peaceful growth of Cheshire's population and wealth it has left few individual remains of exceptional interest. But Vale Royal is an outstanding monastic site in a splendid setting which has not yet been fully investigated.

The structure of the inner core of some of Cheshire's most interesting old towns such as Nantwich, Macclesfield and Congleton, was probably formed during this period. It survives in the street patterns, the position and sometimes the fabric of a few major buildings like churches, and numbers of hidden remains and indications still to be investigated by excavation. For instance, the position of Nantwich Castle has been strongly suggested, and medieval remains of great potential interest, in clearly defined strata which may cast fresh light on the history of the town, were discovered in August 1974.

Similarly, an interesting village such as Malpas owes much of its present form to development during the 12th, 13th and 14th centuries. The medieval street patterns may tell as much as the position, date and nature of the surviving buildings (church, castle and tithebarn) of the medieval form and function of this, as other villages.

From 1400 to the dissolution of the Monasteries

Prosperity and parish churches.

The 15th century brought growing prosperity on the land, at least for the landowners, and growth of towns and villages, even though the Wars of the Roses (1455-1485) must have interrupted civil progress during thirty years of intermittent fighting. When Henry VII restored peace after the Battle of Bosworth Field, a sudden energy seems to have flowered in Cheshire to secure growing prosperity with building and rebuilding on a new scale. The largest remaining legacy from this period is in many of the churches in town and country parishes, some of them very fine.

Manors and cottages; agriculture.

Very little remains from this or earlier periods of the cottages or small houses of labourers or craftsmen; but while Chorley Old Hall is probably the only hall remaining with work from before the 15th century, a number of manors and halls from the 15th and early 16th centuries survive; for instance, Bewsey Old Hall, Warrington, parts of Gawsworth Hall, Gawsworth Old Rectory, the great hall of Little Moreton Hall and the roof of Tatton Old Hall.

The relatively wet climate and the large areas of forest heavily influenced farming in Cheshire. It was poor corn country and crops of wheat, barley and oats were grown only to meet local needs. For the same reasons stock-rearing flourished, mainly cattle and pigs but not sheep. Cheshire was already a noted producer of cheese, sold outside the county. It could stand the lengthy journey to the larger, southern, urban markets without deterioration. There was some agricultural improvement including a measure of enclosure — but to consolidate holdings for arable and pasture rather than the widespread enclosure ascribed to sheep farming elsewhere in England (see T. Driver op cit Ch 4(i) and H.J. Hewitt op cit Ch 2). It may well be that some of the oldest hedgerows which still survive (especially along the boundaries of the ancient parishes) date from this period.

The Bridge, Farndon, 1345.

St Mary's Church, Nantwich — 14th century Decorated tower.

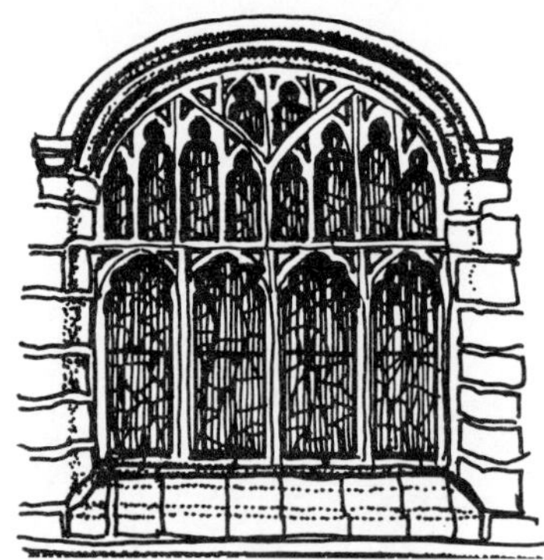

St Oswald's Church, Malpas — Perpendicular aisle window, about 1500.

Little Moreton Hall, 15th century Great Hall — closely spaced pre-Tudor oak framing.

The Moat, Little Moreton Hall — decorative rather than defensive.

A cruck framed cottage.

Restored medieval gatehouse, Bradley Old Hall, Burtonwood, Warrington.

49 Bridge Street Row, Chester — old St Michael's Rectory, mid 17th century.

Great Budworth Church on the village skyline.

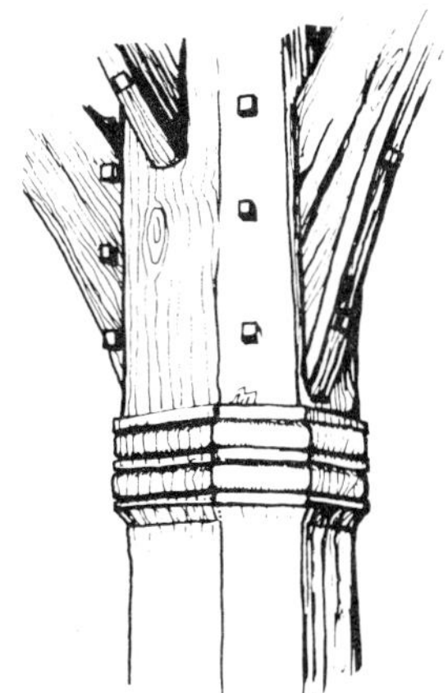

St Oswald's Church, Lower Peover — detail of oak column and bracketed arch 13th or 14th century.

In the towns, little that is obvious remains of houses and workshops or shops from this period, but in quieter centres such as Congleton where buildings were refaced rather than renewed during the 18th and 19th centuries a good deal of medieval work may lurk behind newer facades, and in Chester there are remains, often hidden from the streets, in the lower storeys of some buildings in the town centre.

The Port of Chester.

Chester complained of the progressive silting up of the Dee and the reduction of shipping in the port; but this claim generally was used to justify appeals to reduce the burden of taxes levied on the city, and the degree of its truth is disputed by historians. The harbours further down the estuary towards the open sea were all part of the port of Chester, so that dues on shipping would not altogether be lost to the City if the other harbours were used by the larger ships. Indeed, the Dee estuary remained the principal port in north-west England for coastal trade, trade with Ireland and trade at least in metals and wine with continental Europe. Liverpool was not yet dominant, or even independent. Its harbour had been used at least from the 13th century, but under the jurisdiction of the Port of Chester until 1647. The 17th century saw the beginning of its rapid modern growth.

Comment

Enough remains of castles and of Chester's fortifications to illustrate Cheshire's military importance in the Middle Ages. Medieval roads and the port of Chester, including harbours such as Shotwick further down the estuary, have left hardly a trace above ground, vital though they were. Some sort of picture can be reconstructed of the monasteries and the place they played in medieval society. Of parish churches, sufficient have survived from the later Middle Ages to make clear the part they played not only in worship but in education and entertainment and as centres of social life and repositories of records and commemorative monuments. There are no surviving early medieval dwellings and even until the 16th century very little indeed except the larger houses which were the halls and manors. Sites of subsequently deserted medieval villages exist in fairly large numbers in Cheshire and there are traces of medieval field patterns and other sites of interest not yet investigated. such as moats.

Chester's Rows, the shopping galleries at first floor level in the old streets of the city centre are a unique legacy of the Middle Ages. They may have developed as the level of the streets, gradually rising with successive repairs, left the original ground floors rather lower than the streets and made staircase access to the first floors from the pavements easier. The two-level shopping centre which has emerged still contributes to Chester's commercial success by concentrating so much activity in a compact centre.

The churches offer one of the greatest problems for conservation amongst the surviving buildings because of the scale and expense of restoration work which is necessary — even allowing for the limited aid proposed by Central Government.

Cheshire has a unique and historically important heritage of oak-framed churches. Lower Peover is one of the best examples.

The investigation of medieval documents and the study of aerial photographs are showing more and more clearly that remains which now lie below ground (including a number of deserted medieval villages) should be able to tell much of life, society and work in medieval Cheshire.

Monument to Randle Brereton and his wife, 1522, St Oswald's Church, Malpas.

16th. and 17th. Century Buildings

16th and 17th century cottages at Great Budworth.
Good husbandry brought rural prosperity which
encouraged much building in villages and countryside.

High Street, Nantwich. The Crown Hotel
was originally a private town house. The
whole town centre had to be rebuilt after
the disastrous fire of 1583 but the
medieval street pattern and much of
archaeological interest below ground
remain.

Nether Alderley Mill, probably a 17th
century building on a medieval mill site.
Machinery 19th century. Water mills were
a vital feature of the rural economy up to
the beginning of the railway age.

Great Budworth Old School in the
Churchyard dates from about 1600.

Mid 17th century almshouses Park Street, Chester, restored by the City Council.

Audlem Grammar School 1652; perhaps the best example of a 17th century grammar school in Cheshire.

The Eagle and Child cottage, Nether Alderley; probably built as an inn, it became a staging point for post-horses during the coaching age and is now a private house.

Cottages at Prestbury probably of the 17th century. Gritstone is a common building material on the east Cheshire Plain and foothills adjoining the Pennines.

Following the dissolution of the monasteries Henry VIII sold most of the monastic lands to families who have owned and improved their rural estates over the succeeding centuries.

The mill pond forms an ornamental moat to the Manor House at Nether Alderley.

The Bluecoat School Chester, originally a school for orphans, illustrates the scope of practical benefactions during the 18th century.

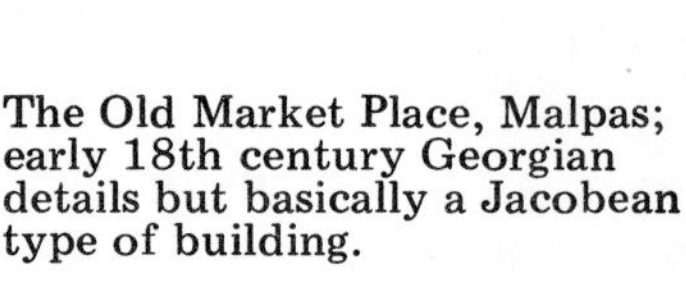

The Old Market Place, Malpas; early 18th century Georgian details but basically a Jacobean type of building.

17th century embellishment to the medieval castle at **Doddington near Nantwich.**

The earliest farm houses and farm buildings commonly to survive in use in Cheshire date from the 17th and 18th centuries. An example near Peover.

The Castle Hotel, Halton was built as a courthouse by the Duchy of Lancaster.

Rebuilding and refacing of old buildings and much new building transformed the character of many old towns during the 18th century.

Welsh Row, Nantwich.

Bank Hall, Warrington. A magnificent town house by James Gibbs — now the Town Hall.

Abbey Square, Chester.

Cottages at Knutsford probably built by the Lords Egerton of Tatton.

Cheshire from 1540 to 1750

From the dissolution of the Monasteries to the Canal Age

Two events which radically changed the flow of life in Cheshire were the dissolution of the monasteries in the 1540's and the genesis of economic heavy inland transport which came with the cutting of the artifical canals during the second half of the 18th century.

The dissolution of the monasteries caused the destruction of three of the largest and finest medieval building groups in the county — Norton Priory, Vale Royal Abbey and Combermere Abbey — together with their dependencies. More fundamentally it changed the whole pattern of land ownership, destroyed an important agency of road repair and maintenance and, together with Henry VIII's break with Rome, encouraged the growing emphasis on secular objectives in society, thought and the economy.

From the dissolution to the Civil War: 1540 to 1642

Oak-framed Jacobethan house, Prestbury, now the National Westminster Bank.

Oak framed "black-and-white" houses begin to give way to early classical designs in stone and brick.

The first fruit of this new growth was the proliferation of oak-framed houses. A good deal survives; new large houses in the countryside, extensions to old halls and manors and a number of buildings in the streets of old towns and villages (sometimes hidden behind later brick fronts). Henry VIII sold the monastic lands which the Crown had acquired to the peaceful rural landowners whose interest has been the progressive consolidation and improvement of their estates. They seem to have set to with vigour to improve countryside and towns as soon as the land was theirs.

Hospital Street, Nantwich — 17th century doorway and windows embellish an earlier house.

The oak-framed houses — similar in all but detail and greater opulence to those which had been built before the Dissolution — are essentially late medieval country houses, friendly, informal and unsophisticated. Parallel with the continuance of the tradition of timber-framed building (common to the Border counties from Chester to Chepstow, where oak trees provided the readiest building material to hand), imposing brick and stone houses, showing the first faltering attempts at classicism, began to appear — Brereton Hall south of Holmes Chapel and, more ambitiously, Lyme Park. A little later, at the beginning of the 17th century, brick was used impressively in the fine Jacobean Halls of Crewe and Dorfold.

In Chester and Nantwich, and to a lesser extent elsewhere, a number of good half-timbered town houses from the late 16th and the 17th century survive, side by side with the brick which superseded timber framing, as a rule, by 1700.

Monument to Dame Alice Fitton, Gawsworth Church, 1627.

Inns, schools, almshouses, windmills and water mills.

A greater variety of building began to emerge in the 17th century; for instance inns recognisably built as such, schools and almshouses. The old Grammar School at Audlem (1652) is an excellent example.

Wind and water mills were common in the Middle Ages, usually for grinding corn. Transport of heavy produce over long distances was laborious and expensive, except by sea or navigable rivers, so that corn mills had to be local, and consequently small. Chester, the biggest town in the region and a main port and centre of communications, at least since Norman times, had a larger mill on the north side of the Dee by the weir. Examples of water mill buildings survive from the 16th century onward. Nether Alderley Mill (restored by the National Trust) in east Cheshire and Stretton Mill in west Cheshire (in course of restoration by Cheshire County Council) are among the best examples. The oldest surviving mill machinery, at Stretton Mill, south east of Farndon, dates from the 18th century.

Lyme Park; the Elizabethan north front attempting classical composition, 1570.

Farming and the countryside.

Of farming and the countryside, information is scanty, but, to judge from the record of complaints by cavalry commanders during the Civil War, Cheshire's farmland was fairly commonly enclosed by 1640, and divided by hedges which the horses could not jump. In the grounds of the great houses like Lyme Park, the deliberate creation of ornamental landscape was to come later. During the 16th and 17th century they appear to have been valued by their owners chiefly as deer-parks, good venues for hunting.

Lyme Cage, Lyme Park — an Elizabethan hunt observation tower.

The Civil War

The Civil War must have brought development in Cheshire to a halt for more than ten years, with constant military activity in the countryside, a few pitched battles (notably Rowton Moor, and Nantwich, where the field was by Acton), and the long siege of Chester. It was the last time that medieval fortifications were used in England. The walls of Chester were evidently an effective defence, but the garrison of Beeston Castle were surprised and overcome by a group of the enemy who climbed the rock and got in through the kitchens.

Where new defences were needed (as at Nantwich), earthworks were thrown up, rather than stone walls. But the destruction to our heritage brought on by the war was to the medieval sculpture and paintings on and in the churches, rather than to secular buildings. Indeed, there are links between the religious disputes which contributed to the 17th century Civil War and the sectarian aspect of the violence in 20th century Ulster.

Roads and bridges fell into serious disrepair for no one had replaced the monasteries as an effective agency for their management and maintenance, and the wars stopped such work as the parishes had undertaken.

Military activity; civil stagnation; destruction.

The late 17th and early 18th Centuries

There are few individually noteworthy remains from the last decades of the 17th century or from the early 18th century. The Unitarian Chapels at Knutsford, Dean Row and Macclesfield — the first Non-Conformist churches in Cheshire — of around 1690 were Jacobean in character. On a grand scale, Leoni's substantial work at Lyme Park (1720's) was Cheshire's first major taste of the classical style, but even here more with a 17th than an 18th century character. The Bluecoat School at Chester (1717) is important as a mark of the growing use of private charitable funds for social purposes, here an orphanage as well as a school, not only for its architectural quality.

Chapels, country houses, schools, almshouses, orphanages.

The most widespread characteristic of the late 17th and early 18th century, on the evidence of remaining buildings, was the development and improvement of farms and farmland. Surviving farmhouses and farm buildings from this period in Cheshire can be measured by hundreds; and it is the first period to leave a substantial legacy of cottages in the countryside and villages.

Farms and farmland.

Chester steadily sank in importance as a port; Parkgate took its place for the Irish trade, and Liverpool began to grow as a major port. But this meant change of emphasis rather than eclipse for Chester. Its importance as a market centre for West Cheshire and North Wales, as a garrison town and as an ecclesiastical, administrative and judicial centre remained.

Chester's changing role.

Button-making was an organised industry in Macclesfield from the 17th century, but organised by contractors who farmed out the work to craftsmen who had their workshops in their own homes.* But on this domestic basis, the making of copper buttons and the covering of them with silk, the beginning of the silk industry in Cheshire developed. In the early 18th century machinery which could be operated in series by the power of water wheels was developed for the thread-making processes of the textile industry. This, the birth of the factory system, was introduced to Cheshire by Charles Roe, who opened his first silk mill in Macclesfield in 1743.

Macclesfield and the birth of the modern silk industry.

*Now the Japanese are making zips at Runcorn; world-wide distribution of light articles has become possible.

Cromwell's statue, Warrington, 1899, by John Bell of Kensington.

Detail of Wright's Almshouses, Nantwich, 1638.

School in Nether Alderley churchyard, 1693.

Queen Anne doorway, Chestergate, Macclesfield, the home of Charles Roe, founder of the local silk industry.

The salt industry in the Weaver Valley.

The salt industry began to see change. The old brine springs could no longer satisfy the demand, so wells and pits were dug to increase supplies, and the pumping of brine from shafts sunk into the wet rock began before the end of the 17th century.

In 1682 the first recorded mine was opened to dig dry rock salt at Marbury. Salt was still mainly used to preserve seasonal food (especially meat) and in traditional craft industries such as tanning. Rock salt had to be purified by solution and evaporation, but this was relatively economical because salt in the natural brine was in a weaker solution.

The development of pumping and of rock salt mines in the northern part of the salt field presaged the ultimate eclipse of Nantwich by Northwich, Middlewich, Winsford and Sandbach. Early in the 17th century Nantwich had produced twice as much salt as Middlewich and three times as much as Northwich.

Comment

The main legacy of the Elizabethan, Jacobean and early Georgian periods is the country houses, town houses, farm buildings and the progressive improvement and enclosure of the countryside. Conservation of the buildings may offer problems because of their number, but most at risk appear to be the farm buildings and the characteristics of the farmed landscape which may originate from these periods.

Oak-framed house, Marbury, 16th to 17th century.

Hale Manor near Widnes, Queen Anne classicism (1710).

The Falcon Inn, Lower Bridge Street, Chester.

The Imprint of the 18th. and Early 19th. Centuries on the Rural Scene

Toft Hall Park near Knutsford.

Much of the surviving planting, hedges, trees, copses and deciduous woodland was planted in the 18th and early 19th century.

Farm buildings at Gawsworth.

The Toll-roads of the coaching age brought vastly improved communications.

Toll-house, Kelsall.

The Swan, Tarporley, a Coaching Hotel.

A canal-side corn mill, Christleton. This was originally a steam mill.

Textile Mills predominated in the first phase of the industrial revolution. Corn was still milled in the small scale water and windmills in the countryside.

Wind cornmill, Neston.

Quarry Bank Mill, Styal 1783. The cotton mill and village were built by the proprietor, Samuel Greg who came to Cheshire from Belfast.

Styal; cottages in the 18th century mill village.

The Shot Tower, Chester Leadworks. The metal industries adopted the factory system and early mass production methods during the 18th century.

Thomas Harrison

Thomas Harrison was a Chester architect. His work vies in quality with that of his better known London colleagues.

Officer's Mess, Castle Square, Chester. Harrison designed the square and all the classical buildings which surround it.

Grosvenor Bridge, Chester. A noble single arch stone bridge said to be the largest stone arch in the world when it was built.

Knutsford, St. John Baptist. One of a number of churches rebuilt in the 18th century.

The Sunday School, Macclesfield, 1813. An early and large school erected from public subscription.

18th. Century Public Buildings

Progress, Expansion and Change

Progress covered so many fields of activity during the 18th century that it is difficult to separate cause and effect between the developments in each field. Agricultural improvement brought more food; advances in medical knowledge and hygiene (especially, for the first time, the cheap manufacture of soap) lengthened life expectancy and helped the population to increase; the construction of artificial canals made the economic transport of bulky goods possible: the development of machinery and power for pumps and ventilation enabled the mining of coal and ores to expand — both the industries as a whole and the size of individual mines; the application of water power to newly invented process machinery began to concentrate manufacture in closely grouped factories so as to improve the economy of transport and build up the necessary range of skills. These changes set the scene for the progressive shift of population from countryside and villages to the towns.

Agriculture and the Countryside

Improvement of soil and implements. A new class of farmer.

Nationally, the second half of the 18th century saw a growth of understanding of the chemistry of the soil, and of scientific means of improving it. With the growth of understanding came also the rapid improvement of farm implements; and in many parts of the country the enclosure of land (which had been tilled in common) took place on a scale which had substantial social consequences— the replacement of the peasant farmer (who had tilled the land with simple implements and almost no capital, largely to provide his own subsistence) by the larger farmer (whether tenant or landowner) who had also to be a manager, an employer of labour and a producer of goods for the market.

Farm and farmbuildings

Land drainage; trees and hedges; rural parkland.

Rural Cheshire may have changed less radically than the arable counties during the 18th century — indeed the most significant change may well have been the least immediately obvious, the great improvement of land drainage. There is evidence that substantial enclosures of Cheshire farmland had occurred in earlier centuries, as had the introduction of long leases for farm holdings. However, this evidence is capable of more than one interpretation and it is clear that the creation of large integrated dairy farms and of ornamental parkland around the country mansions during the 18th and early 19th century have contributed much to the present rural landscape. The subtle harmony which was achieved between the great houses and their ordered but informal landscaped settings is, in Professor Pevsner's view, England's most individual single contribution to European architecture. Much unostentatious planting from the period also remains in the hedgerows and roadside trees, clumps of trees and copses which give variety and interest to the pastoral landscape of the farmland; and in the many fine trees, now mature and over-mature, which grace the villages.

Lyme Park from the saloon — House by Giacomo Leoni c 1720. Harmony of architecture and landscaping.

Deserted villages; obsolete field patterns.

Change often entails destruction, and it may well be that the agricultural development and landscaping of the Georgian and Victorian periods led to the destruction of older villages and field patterns — a subject which has not yet been investigated in Cheshire.

Local builders; architects with country-wide practices.

The farmhouses and farmbuildings of the 18th and 19th century were usually designed by local builders whose names are lost. They are an important part of the local vernacular of traditional building which continued to develop up to the mid 19th century, preserving a variety of constructional details and different building materials between one part of the country and another. By contrast, the 18th century is also the period when the larger houses and public buildings first show a big proportion of designs by leading national architects — most frequently Samuel Wyatt and his nephew Lewis, but with fine examples of John Carr of York's work at Tabley Park and James Gibbs' at Bank Hall, Warrington (now the Town Hall); and with Sir Robert Smirke first introducing 'Gothick' motifs at Cholmondeley Castle. Primarily in a single field, public buildings, the Chester architect Thomas Harrison proved himself as talented a designer as his better known colleagues from London and York.

Tabley House near Knutsford, 1761-7, by John Carr of York.

Brindley's Aqueduct, c 1765,
Bridgewater Canal, Lymm.

"Van Gogh" lift bridge, Llangollen
Branch Canal, Wrenbury.

Canal lockgates and warehouses,
Ellesmere Port.

Many other developments during this period depended on the improvement of transport — roads for passenger traffic, but essentially water for the long distance haulage of all but light and valuable goods. This highlights the importance of Cheshire's position in the national transport system. No county in England can have a better representation of the history of canal building. The improvement of the Mersey and Irwell to provide a route for barges between Liverpool and Manchester was undertaken at the beginning of the 18th century. The navigation (now superseded) passes through the Halton and Warrington districts. Soon after came the deepening and widening of the River Weaver (for salt barges) as far upstream as Northwich. Then, finished in 1757, came England's first artificial canal for the bulk transport of cargo, the St. Helen's canal which opened the South Lancashire coalfield to Manchester and Liverpool via the Mersey and Irwell. Next (1765) came the Cheshire section of the Bridgewater Canal, lockless except for the 'ladder' down to the Mersey at Runcorn (finished 1772). This canal, designed by James Brindley, was built to open up new markets for the Duke of Bridgewater's collieries at Worsley. (Brindley, the first of the great English canal engineers of the 18th century, is reputed to have relied largely on supervising the work on site and to have had little skill at writing). It was to link with the later Trent and Mersey Canal which, with the Shropshire Union and Grand Union canals, joined Cheshire, Liverpool, Manchester and South Lancashire with Birmingham, the main Midlands towns and London later in the century.

The Chester and Ellesmere Port canals, and the Llangollen branch (which were absorbed into the Shropshire Union) and the very late Macclesfield Canal (opened in 1827) were economically more local in impact but their association with Telford as engineer adds to their historic interest.

In some parts of Britain, the 18th century canals were important to the improvement of agriculture because for the first time they provided an economic means of transport for lime, even from distant quarries. If this was relatively unimportant in Cheshire*, the canals did provide a much cheaper and better means of transport of cheese from South Cheshire to London and other large towns.

Textiles were sufficiently valuable in relation to weight and bulk to be less sensitive than many other goods to transport costs and the canal came to Macclesfield and Congleton only twenty years before the railway; but the canals played a crucial part in the development of the salt and the early chemical industries in North Central Cheshire. They served Nantwich less well, and its place as a salt producer had declined sharply by the early 19th century. Consequently it remained a small town, consolidating its position as a rural market centre. This limited the scale of re-development and has enabled it to survive as a town of exceptional archaeological and historic interest. By contrast, the navigations and canals linking St. Helens, Warrington, Widnes, Runcorn, Northwich, Middlewich and Winsford, enabled cheap coal from Lancashire to be applied first to the evaporation of brine in Northwich and Middlewich, and later to the chemical industries which concentrated around Widnes, Warrington, Runcorn and Northwich.

The organ at St. John the Baptist Church at Chester was a barge cargo from London in 1838. It had been at Westminster Abbey and was used at Queen Victoria's Coronation. The canals served special needs as well as the more usual bulk cargoes.

Canals.

Canals and agriculture.

Canals and industry.

Diverse cargoes.

**Local marl had long been used in Cheshire, with similar effects as lime.*

32

Turnpike roads.

Although canals proved to be much the most economic form of transport for heavy and bulky goods, they were generally much too slow to be effective for passenger transport. (There were exceptions. For instance, 'fly-boats' were used during the 19th century between Ellesmere Port and Chester, taking about an hour for the eight mile journey. They were, in principle, a horse-drawn version of the more modern hydrofoil, skimming along the surface of the water instead of cutting through it). So, in parallel with the cutting of the inland waterways, there was the need to improve roads so that they could serve passengers using horse-drawn coaches over long distances. It seems that the social, industrial, and economic developments which were leading to growth of urban population and to increasing centralisation of services and administration, generated an increased demand for personal travel. The improvement of roads and vehicles became imperative. The old parochial administration was unequal to the task of repairing, let alone rebuilding, the main routes, so Turnpike Trusts were set up. They applied the income from the tolls which they charged vigorously and effected the most radical improvement of road planning and construction in Cheshire since Roman days. The famous engineers Telford, Macadam and "Blind Jack" Metcalfe all played their part in the development of Cheshire's highway system and by the early 19th century there were 585 miles of turnpike roads in the County. Apart from the motorways and one or two other new roads they are still the basis of our highway system. In Cheshire the turnpike roads generally followed previously existing routes, but transformed them in character and quality.

Early 19th century bridge over River Weaver, Nantwich.

The Coaching Age — roads and bridges, hotels and toll-houses.

Without the turnpike roads the short, popular coaching age which preceded the growth of the railways could not have flourished. Together, the turnpikes and stage-coaches put fairly remote provincial centres such as Chester within 24 hours of London, and made even longer journeys practicable. For instance, while it had taken eight days to get from Edinburgh to London in 1750, it took less than 48 hours in the 1790's. (Statistical Account of Scotland. Sir John Sinclair, editor 1793-1800).

The outstandingly fine Grosvenor Bridge at Chester designed by Thomas Harrison, a number of lesser bridges and a few surviving toll houses, together with some attractive coaching hotels (notably at Knutsford, but also in other main-road towns) illustrate the improvement in travel facilities in Cheshire.

Entrance to a coaching hotel — The Royal George, Knutsford.

Industry — The Age of Waterpower

Corn and provender mills.

Without the canals, the development of much heavy industry would have been impossible before the railway age, but also they encouraged the establishment of smaller-scale rural industry and warehousing, particularly corn and provender mills; some buildings remain, a reminder that the late 18th and early 19th century were the heyday of the watermill. Previously it had played a vital part in rural life, but transport costs had generally limited the area which a single mill could serve.

Textile mills; the birth of factory industry.

The invention of textile machinery which could be harnessed in series to a single source of power extended the usefulness of the water-wheel to manufacturing industry during the 18th century and introduced the concepts of the factory system and mass production. While the scale of the textile industry in Cheshire was small in relation to Lancashire, it is important because silk preceded cotton and so Macclesfield became a manufacturing town early in the industrial revolution. The same applies on a smaller scale to Congleton. Consequently the interest of these places is that they represent the whole period of the development of the textile industry; they include much of known interest in industrial archaeology and considerable potential for further investigation. Styal is of special interest as an early mill village (two years before the best known of such villages, New Lanark in Clydesdale) where the proprietor provided employment, housing, education and social facilities.

Wheelhouse of textile watermill on Deanbrook, Bollington — this was perhaps the largest water wheel in Cheshire.

Village and mill are now National Trust property.

Weavers' cottages, Lord Street, Macclesfield, with workshops on the top floor.

Entrance, Chester Royal Infirmary, 1761.

Tower of Holy Trinity Church, Warrington — Church 1762, tower 1861.

Detail of Sunderland Street Methodist Church, Macclesfield.

If changes in the late 18th and early 19th centuries were most dramatic in the towns where the mineral and new factory industry concentrated, the steady growth of population, the growth in agricultural production, the improvement of roads and the construction of canals brought growth and a great deal of new building or re-building in the country towns. Much remains from this period in towns which were not then industrial, such as Chester, Knutsford and Sandbach; but similarly in towns with industries such as Warrington and Congleton, a good deal of the building depended on growing trade as much as on industry. In many of these towns the Georgian and Regency periods, taken together, are the most prolific source of buildings listed by the Department of the Environment as being of special architectural or historic interest.

Reasons for growth.

A large proportion of surviving urban buildings from the period were built as houses or shops with living accommodation over, but a number of important buildings show the growth in the range and size of institutions providing for education, the sick, the aged and orphans; for instance, the original buildings of The Chester Royal Infirmary (1761) where, for the first time in England, separate fever wards were built, the main building of Deva Hospital (1827-9), Sir T. Crewe's almshouses at Nantwich, the earlier examples of workhouses, some of which have since become hospitals, and the very large, but rather grim and unadorned Sunday School at Macclesfield (1813). If its pupils were working in the mills, they had no time for school on weekdays and the Sunday school taught reading, writing and arithmetic as well as scripture. New, regularly designed buildings begin during the same period to reflect the development of administration and control — the very fine Shire Hall, courts and military buildings by Thomas Harrison around the Castle Square at Chester (1788-1822); the Sessions House at Knutsford probably by George Moneypenny, although also ascribed to Harrison (1818); Macclesfield Town Hall by Francis Goodwin (1824). In ecclesiastical architecture there was a wave of re-building of parish churches, building of new churches where towns were growing and the building of a number of early Wesleyan chapels.

Shops and houses, hospitals and workhouses; public buildings.

Comment

The scale of building development in towns and villages and the extent and visual quality of the planting and landscaping in the countryside which accompanied the growth of factory industry and the improvement of agriculture during the Georgian and Regency era has left so much which deserves to be conserved that it may pose financial problems. Small 18th and early 19th century houses in pleasant parts of towns, villages and countryside are generally safe enough, but large buildings which have outlived the purpose for which they were built are often very difficult and expensive to convert to new uses. This includes a wide variety of buildings such as schools, mills, churches and early chapels and some country houses. Buildings in town centres are threatened by redevelopment and, decreasingly, by road widening schemes. A careful look is urgently needed at the possibility of restoring and reviving some areas of urban housing from this period which would have disappeared if the less discriminating redevelopment policies of the 1950's and 1960's had continued unaltered.

Buildings.

Countryside.

The hedges and trees of the farmed land and the landscaping and planting of the parks around some of the great country houses probably pose the most acute problems for the next decade. Changing methods of farming do not favour their maintenance or re-planting, and there is no effective national policy or legislation to protect them. Capital transfer tax proposals (March 1975) appear to threaten the continued existence of those large landed estates where landscape and buildings have been designed as part of the total scene. This part of our legacy from the past is most seriously at risk, although a recent survey by the National Trust suggests that it is even more widely valued by Members than are ancient buildings and their contents.

Industry.

The 18th century textile mills were the heralds of the massive industrialisation to come in the 19th century which was so radically to change English towns and urban life, and thus are of special historic significance. Little of the 18th century industrial machinery and equipment have survived, but there is still good evidence, particularly in Macclesfield, Congleton and Styal, of the changes which the mills brought to the way of life of the people who relied on them for work. The rehabilitation and maintenance of the buildings and their environs deserve constant care.

Cheavely Hall Farm, near Aldford — dying trees need replacement, to maintain the fine landscape.

Hoofield Hall, Burton-by-Tarvin

The Anderton Barge Lift, near Northwich, 1875, raises and lowers barges between the river Weaver and the Trent and Mersey Canal.

Dutton Viaduct, Grand Junction Railway,
engineers Stephenson and Locke.

Chester Railway Station, 1847-8.
Architect Francis Thompson.

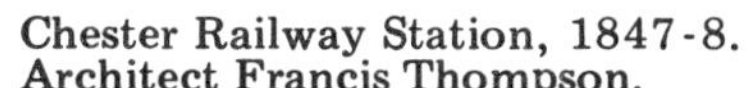

The Railway Viaduct across the Mersey estuary at
Runcorn Gap 1863-8, (engineer W Baker), and the
road viaduct, 1960's, (engineers Mott, Hay and
Anderson).

19th. Century Gardens, Villages Suburbs and Almshouses

Lumley Place, Chester. The Grosvenor family provided dwellings for their retired employees.

Harthill, a village built for the employees on the Bolesworth estate, 1844.

Tatton Park "Chinese" Garden. The bridge was imported from Japan, 1902.

The Iron Gates at Bank Hall, Warrington. Mid 19th century.

Main Street, Halton, a typical village street where 19th century buildings predominate.

Dixon's Houses, Almshouses at Christleton, JO Scott, Architect.

Alderley Edge; one of the large early "commuter" houses.

Christchurch, built by stages as the 19th century railway town developed. It was probably designed by John Cunningham in 1843 but periodically enlarged up to 1906. The tower is by JW Stansby, engineer on the railway company's staff. The church is now redundant and a suitable secular use for it is being sought.

Detail of the Municipal Buildings, 1902, architect JT Hare.

Railway Offices

The Salt Industry

One of the few remaining terraces of railwaymen's cottages.

The Lion Saltworks, Wincham near Northwich. The only old salt pumping plant still in use.

Chester Town Hall 1864-9;
architect WH Lynn of Belfast.

The Old Town Hall, Knutsford; architect
Alfred Waterhouse, 1870 now used as a
furniture showroom.

19th century Bank Offices, Churchyardside,
Nantwich. Alfred Waterhouse designed the
building on the right.

The Queen's School, Chester, 1882, architect
EA Ould a pupil of John Douglas.

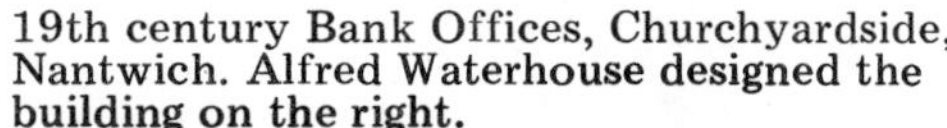

Village School, Tilston Fearnall.
Apparently built by the Tollemaches
of Peckforton Castle, mid 19th
century.

Cast iron bevel gears in an old Cheshire water mill.

Old forge bellows, Wistaston Mill, Crewe.

The Agents of Change

The power of coal and steam made the economic and industrial differences between Georgian and Victorian England possible. Coal had been important to the development and success of industry in the 18th century not because steam yet provided a significant proportion of the motive power for machinery, but because towns could not develop without coal cheap enough for domestic hearths and ovens. The early water-wheel stage of the industrial revolution stimulated the metal industries to provide iron castings for machinery, and ironworks and foundries needed a great deal of coal.

Coal, steam and iron.

Coal was only economical if the mines were close by or if it could be carried cheaply to more distant users by sea or canal. This economic limitation has strongly influenced the main locations of industrial growth in Britain, and generally the pattern was set before the railway age began. The South Lancashire, North Staffordshire and North Welsh coalfields overlap the boundaries of Cheshire. The former mines at Poynton and Macclesfield, Mow Cop, Scholar Green and Neston influenced local developments in the 19th century, but the South Lancashire coalfield has been of greater and more lasting importance, including the coal seams north of the Mersey which Cheshire has inherited from Lancashire in the revision of county boundaries of 1974. It provided fuel for the development of the salt industry and the 19th century chemical industry along the Weaver and Mersey Valleys.

To serve the industrialisation of Victorian England coal, steam and iron needed the vigour and genius of the physicists, chemists and engineers whose discoveries and inventions made the transformation possible. The leading mechanical and civil engineers such as the inventors of textile machinery, and Watt, George and Robert Stephenson, Telford and Brunel, are well enough known. It is less widely appreciated how far the new industries and the radical improvements in farming depended upon the physics of Newton and his colleagues of the Royal Society in 17th century London and the many discoveries of the pioneers of modern chemistry in the 18th and early 19th centuries.

Physicists, chemists and engineers

The conservatism of Oxford and Cambridge towards new subjects of study in the 18th century meant that the torch of scientific and practical research in Britain largely passed to those Scottish universities which stood within the largest cities, where the benefits to be won from the improvement of agriculture and of industrial processes were most clearly seen — Edinburgh, Glasgow and Aberdeen. In England the only colleges which shared in this impetus were the dissenters' academies, one of which was at Warrington. Amongst the distinguished lecturers at the Warrington Academy was Joseph Priestley, best known for the discovery of oxygen. (He was also, for a period, Unitarian minister at Nantwich. His chapel, now demolished, stood at the corner of Hospital Street and Pratchett's Row). Priestley is the first of three chemists who deserve mention here. He played a part in the study of the chemistry of plants and plant growth and was the first to postulate the complementary parts played by the animal and vegetable kingdoms in their use of the air, each exhaling the gases which the other uses. Two other chemists who deserve mention for the impact of their discoveries on the development of North Cheshire are Leblanc, the French chemist who, in the late 18th century, devised the first practical industrial process for making soda in bulk from mineral sources, and Ludwig Mond whose efforts in Cheshire to improve the soda and allied processes were a landmark in the growth of our modern chemical industry.

Main agents of change in Victorian and Edwardian Cheshire were the railways and the Ship Canal, the change and growth of the salt and chemical industries and the vigorous improvement of the rural estates around the great country houses.

The coming of railways reinforced Cheshire's position as a main focus of communications. They have left a heritage of lines and structures no less comprehensive than that of the earlier canals in the county. The recent re-drawing of the county boundaries has brought a small part of the original Manchester and Liverpool railway into Cheshire. This was the world's first railway company owning track, motive power and rolling stock — the first public railway. The world's earliest major railway viaduct* (designed by George Stephenson and his assistant Locke, and built in 1827) across the valley of the Sankey Brook near Newton-le-Willows is now partly in Cheshire and partly in the St. Helen's district of Merseyside. The Grand Junction Railway from Birmingham to Warrington followed in 1837 to provide connections from the Midlands to the Liverpool and Manchester line. The Grand Junction line was of special significance as the first major link in the main north-western route from London and the Midlands to the large Lancashire towns, Carlisle, Glasgow and Edinburgh. The main Cheshire viaducts on this line over the Weaver at Dutton and Vale Royal are especially fine. The design of these great stone bridges is clearly related to the earlier and less assured Sankey Viaduct by the same engineers. (Principally Joseph Locke. He found it difficult to work with the aging Stephenson, and this part of the engineering work was consequently left in his hands). The viaducts by Stephenson and Locke set the pattern of design usually adopted on later railways throughout Britain, except where longer spans were needed than could be built in masonry. Brunel was perhaps the only engineer to better Stephenson and Locke's work with his long, shallow, semi-elliptical brick arches carrying the Great Western line over the Thames at Maidenhead and Goring.

The design of railway bridges in stone and brick benefitted from the long tradition of building large bridges in those materials, going back to the Roman aqueducts in Western Europe. The engineers understood their materials and their bridges seldom failed. By contrast, iron was a new material and locomotives were a dangerous load which could set up disastrous vibrations in an inappropriate structure. Even Robert Stephenson, engineer of the brilliant tubular Britannia Bridge over the Menai Straits, committed a serious error at Chester. The semi-suspension design of his iron bridge over the Dee was unsuitable to carry locomotives, and collapsed tragically under a moving train.

The later railways, generally more of regional or local significance in the national network, continued to grow through the second third of the 19th century. They provide interesting examples of the development of engineering from the massive brick viaducts of the old North Staffordshire railway at Congleton and North Rode (1849, J.C. Forsyth) to the ornate high Victorian iron viaduct across the Mersey estuary at Runcorn Gap (W. Baker, Engineer, 1863/8) and the 20th century steel transporter bridge by Sir William Arrol & Co. (the builders of the Forth Bridge) over the Mersey to sidings at Joseph Crosfields works at Warrington (1913).

Baker's Mersey Viaduct has all the confident competence of a mid-Victorian engineer's work, yet there was another side to his working life; he had been nicknamed "General Baker" for his success in leading gangs of navvies in inter-company disputes.

Chester became an important railway junction where the lines of several rival companies met; at first they worked in something less than harmony, sharing the very fine station designed by Francis Thompson (with work by Robert Stephenson and C.H. Wild) built in 1847/8.

Congleton Viaduct, 1849, engineer JC Forsyth (former N Staffs Railway).

Sankey Brook viaduct — the Liverpool and Manchester Railway over the St. Helens Canal.

Signal box, Mouldsworth Junction (former Cheshire Lines Railway).

The railways, the Manchester Ship Canal (opened 1894) and on a lesser scale the successive improvements of the Weaver Navigation for seagoing ships influenced not only the development of industry in and around Cheshire, but also the growth of the towns and the distribution of population in the County. Commercially, the Manchester Ship Canal was substantially a Cheshire venture, backed by Lord Egerton of Tatton, who was related to the Duke of Bridgewater. The census of population, taken at 10-yearly intervals from 1801, give an outline of the changes: —

High Street, Bollington — a small Victorian Pennine-foot cotton town.

Edwardian houses, Alsager, for Pottery managers who commuted by train to Stoke-on-Trent.

(i) The towns which remained primarily centres of trade and services for the rural population grew slowly but steadily; Chester, Knutsford, Sandbach and Nantwich together had about 33,000 inhabitants in 1831 but 58,000 by 1911. — **Country towns.**

(ii) During the same period the salt towns of the Weaver Valley which later attracted the chemical industries of Brunner and Mond (Northwich, Winsford and Middlewich) grew from about 11,000 to nearly 34,000. The chemical towns on the Mersey grew even more strongly; Widnes from 2,000 to 31,500; Warrington from 16,000 to 72,000, and Runcorn from about 5,500 to 17,400. — **Salt and chemical industry towns.**

(iii) By contrast, the 18th century textile towns, Macclesfield and Congleton, remained more or less as they had been; consequently a good deal of their 18th century development has survived. Bollington grew largely as a small 19th century cotton mill town, and it still retains much of the Victorian character of its layout and buildings in a pleasant Pennine-foot setting. — **Textile towns.**

(iv) The Grand Junction Railway Company created Crewe entirely as the centre of their administration and workshops. Where there had been only 148 inhabitants in 1831 there were 45,000 by 1901. Although not a company town like Crewe, Ellesmere Port depended for its growth largely on the Ship Canal. The area to be occupied by the town held some 1,500 people in 1881, but it was a town of 10,400 by 1901. The coming of the oil-based industries has contributed to a second burst of growth, dependent on the canal, in recent years. — **Crewe and Ellesmere Port.**

(v) The railways encouraged the first commuter suburbs and towns. If boundary changes have lost Cheshire most such settlements which depended for employment on Manchester, Liverpool and Stoke-on-Trent, she still has three — Wilmslow (growth from 5,700 in 1881 to 8,200 in 1911), Alsager (growth from some 700 in 1861 to 2,600 in 1901) and Alderley Edge. As a "commuter settlement" Alderley Edge is of particular interest. In 1841 there was a village of 560 people. By 1861 this had grown to 1,760. The growth resulted from the efforts of the railway company to attract merchants and managers working in Manchester to live in a rural setting adjoining the line so that they would travel to and from work by rail. As a bait, new residents were offered a period of free first class daily return travel to Manchester. The upshot was the rapid growth of a unique settlement of large and often finely designed "romantic" houses set informally in an interesting, steeply sloping, well wooded landscape on land which the railway company had provided for the purpose. The houses include work by some eminent architects of the late 19th and early 20th century. — **Suburbs and commuter towns.**

(vi) By the end of the 19th century the railways provided a fairly close network of lines (which has now been cut back) to serve many of the needs of agriculture, rural industry and short distance passenger transport. — **The countryside.**

The Salt and Chemical Industries

The development in Cheshire of the industries which the 19th century railways served and encouraged centred on salt and chemicals in the Weaver and Mersey Valleys, but with more diverse industry at Warrington, and coal mining north of the Mersey. The design of industrial plant constantly changes and improves, and the old is scrapped to make way for the new. Remains of plant or machinery which has been superseded are consequently almost impossible to find except where factories have been abandoned without redevelopment. There are one or two such sites in Cheshire — perhaps most notably Spike Island at Widnes and old salt workings around Northwich. The 19th century chemical works in North Cheshire were significant to the development of our national economy. Brunner and Mond founded enterprises which were a cradle of England's modern chemical industry.

Remains of Hutchinsons No 1 Soda Works at Widnes, possibly lime kilns, 1847.

Raw materials and processes.

The heavy inorganic chemical industry relied on three main raw materials: — salt, limestone and pyrites (for sulphuric acid), and burnt a great deal of fuel. Salt came from the Weaver Valley, limestone from Derbyshire, and pyrites from the Pennines. Fuel came mainly from the South Lancashire coalfield.

Nearly a hundred years before the modern chemical industry began to develop in North Cheshire, some of its industrial customers, glassworks and textile bleachers and dyers, had begun to establish themselves in South Lancashire. Two major soapworks were founded early in the 19th century — Joseph Crosfield's in 1814 at Warrington and Gossage's. During the 18th century and the first three decades of the 19th century most of the raw materials for these industries (except sand and lead in the glass industry) were organic, and some of them were bizarre. Kelp (burned seaweed), wood-ash, barilla (the ash of a Mediterranean plant). sour milk, cow dung and human urine (sometimes distilled to produce ammonia) are examples which show how great was the advance when chemicals began to be synthesised from mineral resources. Proportions of the useful chemicals obtained from the old plant and animal sources were very low; for that reason and because the chemistry of the active reagents only slowly came to be understood, the processes were highly inefficient. For instance, 1000 lbs of dry seaweed cut laboriously from the rocky coast of the Hebrides and burnt on the seashore to give 150 lbs of kelp, then shipped to Liverpool, might yield only 6 lbs of potash for the soap makers. The end products were consequently expensive and so used with great economy. Following the industrial revolution processes have become efficient, products cheap, and their use profligate.

Dry seaweed; 1,000 lbs.

Kelp; 150 lbs.

Potash; 5 lbs.

Salt.

For the new industries, salt was the raw material indigenous to Cheshire which grew in importance for the production of other bulk chemicals. Salt was already exported from the Weaver Valley to the Netherlands and North America, but as these countries began to develop their own resources and exports declined, the growing demand for soda and "saltcake" called for increased production.

Industries dependent on salt or its derivatives are grouped in the Mersey and Weaver Valleys, South Lancashire and North Staffordshire — the Mond Division of ICI at Widnes, Runcorn and Northwich; great soap works and chemical works at Warrington and Bebington; glass at St. Helens and elsewhere in South Lancashire; the Lancashire textile industries and salt-glazed earthenware and stone-ware in North Staffordshire and South Cheshire.

The structure of the salt industry changed as its plant became more complex, expensive and efficient, and as the producers grew in size and tended to merge with their largest and nearest customers, the chemical works. At first, the rock salt mines and the brine salt works were numerous, particularly along the banks of the Weaver between Northwich and Winsford and around Northwich, and mostly small. Apparently they were sometimes poorly equipped and managed. The flooding of mines was fairly frequent and fierce competition between the salt works led, through severe price cutting, to bankruptcies. The subsequent reorganisation (first through the only partly successful cartel, the Salt Union and then, as capital needs increased, the dominance of the industry by a few big firms) has brought a very different pattern — a much smaller number of large works, and a single rock-salt mine at Winsford.

Soap Works from Bank Quay station, Warrington — here Joseph Crofield started soap making in 1814.

During the first two-thirds of the 19th century the heavy inorganic chemical industry relied on the two-stage process which Leblanc had patented in France in 1791. Leblanc had begun to develop his process commercially, financed by the Duke of Orleans, just before the French revolution, but their success was shortlived. The Duke died on the guillotine and Leblanc, thus deprived of capital, later took his own life in a French workhouse. The process was first to react common salt (sodium chloride) with sulphuric acid to produce saltcake (sodium sulphate) and hydrochloric acid. The saltcake was then "balled" with coke and lime in a hand-fed furnace to produce soda ash (sodium carbonate), calcium sulphide and carbon dioxide. The soda ash was the most valuable product used in bulk in the soap, textile and glass industries, although the intermediate product, saltcake, was also used in glass making. Industrial uses for hydrochloric acid were not at first available. It was released into the air for many years as a corrosive vapour, with dire results for men, beasts, trees and grassland. Later, William Gossage of St. Helens, devised scrubbing towers which were built to trap the vapour. The towers contained screens of brushwood or coke over which water fell to absorb the rising gas, and so form hydrochloric acid.

The Leblanc process; soda ash and saltcake for bleaching, soap-making and glass-making.

A Leblanc process works was first set up in England on Tyneside in 1814, but a few years later (1822) Muspratt built a works at Liverpool. In 1829 Widnes Dock opened, and in 1833 completion of the St. Helens and Runcorn Gap railway meant that Widnes, a small, marshy, agricultural village, had access to the South Lancashire coalfield by water and railway and to Pennine limestone by canal. The dock, built by the railway company, was probably the world's first railway dock. By 1847 John Hutchinson had seen the opportunity which Widnes offered — cheap land and good access to coal and raw materials — and built his first works there, using the Leblanc process. He recruited much of his work force from Ireland — people seeking surer food and employment following the Irish potato famine of 1846/7. Widnes soon became an example of the disadvantages of the Leblanc process; severe aerial pollution from the hydrochloric acid waste gases and the need for large areas of land for the dumping of the semi-solid alkali waste or "galligu". The rapid growth of the town without sewerage or piped water services made it a prey to epidemic disease. To this scene came John Brunner, who worked for Hutchinson, and the chemist, Ludwig Mond, who sought to persuade Hutchinson to give the improved process which he had devised for recovery of sulphur, a commercial trial. From the subsequent partnership of Brunner and Mond came the development of the Winnington works near Northwich, the cradle of our modern heavy inorganic chemical industry. They introduced the Solvay and electrolytic processes in place of the Leblanc process, improving efficiency and progressively reducing pollution. The Solvay process produces soda ash, electrolysis produces caustic soda, hydrogen, chlorine and sodium. The salt-sulphuric acid process, which is also used, produces saltcake (used in the glass industry) and hydrochloric acid.

The chemical industry at Widnes and Winnington.

Before the first works was built at Widnes, Warrington was already established as an industrial town with metal, clock and toolmaking industries and Greenall's Brewery and Distillery and Walker's Brewery flourishing during the 18th century. Joseph Crosfield introduced soap making in 1814. He was a friend and associate of two other pioneers of the soap industry in the North West, J.C. Gamble and William Gossage, who both lived and worked at St. Helens.

Warrington and Joseph Crosfield.

The nature of the settlements, whether towns, parts of towns or villages, which housed the communities who worked for the new industries or transport companies, varied. Many, such as Warrington, Widnes and Northwich developed or redeveloped continuously over a longish period so that each part of them bears some separate character and identity. Poynton, developed as a colliery village, retains a good deal of its original character; Crewe retains some interesting public buildings, a few original operational buildings of the Grand Junction and London North Western Railway Companies but very little of the original housing built for railway staff and employees. Brunner and Mond built Winnington Village for their employees at the gates of their new chemical works. If not distinguished in design, the village has an interesting place in our industrial history because of the vital part which its founders played in the emergence of Britain's modern chemical industry — and in the development of industrial relations. Dukesfield, on a triangle of land between the Ship Canal, the railway viaduct and the line of the old

Expansion of old towns; growth of new towns and villages.

Entrance to Widnes Dock, 1831, right, and St. Helen's Canal New Cut, 1833, left.

Late 19th century cottages at Winnington, Brunner Mond's model industrial village.

A 19th century house for Bridgewater Canal staff, Dukesfield, Runcorn.

Bridgewater Canal at Runcorn, is one of the best examples of an integrated development within a town — in this case for canal workers — clearly related to its source of employment and still retaining a similar social structure to that of its original community.

The few examples noted in the last paragraph have been "picked out" from the miles of Victorian and Edwardian housing and factories in Cheshire which depended on 19th century industrial expansion, because they are settlements or parts of settlements where the housing and some of the public buildings and community services can clearly be related to specific employers. The history of most development of the period — good, bad and indifferent — is less easy to trace. A fairly large proportion of it has disappeared in post-war redevelopment. Now that rehabilitation is acknowledged to be an alternative to clearance, the specific historic interest and the survival of community ties and pride in areas such as Dukesfield deserve to be given weight when their future is in the balance.

Higher Poynton.

Public Buildings, Public Services and Commercial Development

Public buildings and parks.

As, with the expansion of industry, trade and population, almost every town in Cheshire grew substantially, the need for regulation of development and for public administration and services also grew strongly, first to secure sanitation and health and for policing, for churches, and then for recreation and compulsory education. A good number of the buildings remain; for instance churches, town halls, police stations, hospitals, and schools. But rather than these buildings, perhaps the most valuable, attractive and interesting legacy of the Victorian local authorities and urban landowners to the towns is the ornamental parks. Cheshire has a number which are beautifully designed and sometimes finely sited — Victoria and West Parks at Macclesfield, Grosvenor Park at Chester, the Queen's Park at Crewe and others.

A pub near the colliery village

Town centres; shops and offices.

Just as the foundations were laid during Victoria's reign for much of today's public administration and services, so was the basis of modern trade and commercial services. The layout, land use pattern and appearance of many of the town centres in Cheshire still reflect this influence, but usually with the earlier imprint of the 18th century, and sometimes of the Middle Ages, and, at Chester, the Roman period still traceable behind it.

The Countryside and Villages: The Great Estates and Cheshire Architects

While the 19th century transformed the towns and communications between them, the changes which it brought to the countryside were less dramatic. Improvement of farmland and the renewal of farmhouses and farm buildings continued, the more prosperous villages grew and old buildings there were fairly widely replaced by new. The development with most impact on the rural scene was the consolidation and improvement of the major country estates. The farm management, ornamental landscaping and planting of coverts, the building of new farms designed so as to give the whole estate a coherent style, the rebuilding or new building of whole villages and to some extent the rebuilding or new building of great country houses (most notably Eaton Hall and Peckforton Castle) illustrate the expenditure in the countryside of resources on a scale which could only be built up from metropolitan estates and urban industry.

Old Police Station, Foregate Street, Chester, by John Douglas.

Bandstand in Queen's Park, Crewe, c 1890.

The Grosvenor Estate; Chester and its setting.

The Grosvenor Estate, centred on Eaton Park on the west bank of the Dee, three miles upstream from Chester, is of unusual interest not only because of its size — some 16 square miles of rural land — but for the thoroughness and the integrity of style with which its villages, farms, cottages and landscape were transformed during the second half of the 19th century. While Alfred Waterhouse (a leader of the High Victorian Gothic Revival) designed the Hall, now largely demolished, a band of local architects, notably John Douglas, designed most of the buildings in the estate's model villages, Eccleston, Saighton, Aldford and Pulford, as well as farmhouses and cottages in the countryside and in villages such as Dodleston which impinge on the estate, without being wholly absorbed by it.

Crewe Hall Park; estate cottages by Eden Nesfield, c 1865.

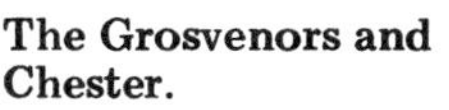

Northgate Street, Chester — detail of late Victorian range, designed by John Douglas and others.

Detail of house by John Douglas, Grosvenor Park Road, Chester, c 1879.

House, Leigh Road, Knutsford, romantically designed by Richard Watt or his associates, c 1900.

A group of estate cottages Eccleston.

The Grosvenors' huge ownership of land in Cheshire included a fair proportion of Chester, almost contiguous with Eaton Park. Thus they were able, by employment of the same architects, to harmonise the style and character of development in the city with that on their parkland and farmland. Interesting in itself, this integration of Victorian Chester with its neighbouring countryside to the south is especially notable for enabling Douglas and his colleagues to develop their talent for reinterpreting the romantic qualities of late medieval and Jacobean domestic building to such great effect. In central Chester, their work closely followed the massing and motifs of the genuine thing — 16th and 17th century oak-framed buildings — but with even more variety of effect and intricacy of carving.

Obviously still highly popular with visitors, Douglas's, Lockwood's and their colleagues' work in Northgate Street, Werburgh Street and Eastgate Street is perhaps the most successful 19th century attempt in England to recreate the character of a medieval town centre. Outside the city centre, Douglas's designs generally express a very free interpretation of the character of buildings from previous centuries, rather than a literal historicism.

The Tatton Estate was associated with Knutsford as closely as the Grosvenor Estate with Chester, but Knutsford is smaller and the impact is therefore on a lesser scale. While the buildings of the architects working for the Grosvenor family deserve a place in the national history of the 19th century Gothic Revival, a small band of designers collaborated at Knutsford to produce a few fascinating groups of individualistic buildings which no exact parallel elsewhere in England. The designers, perhaps headed by R.H. Watt, also included H. Fairhurst of Manchester, Walter Aston, John Brooke, W. Longworth and, at least as a contributor of ideas and comment, Edgar Wood.

If he was eager to borrow motifs from a number of countries and periods to contribute to the design of a single building, Watt appears to have drawn his main inspiration from studying and sketching some of the small medieval towns of Italy. The buildings which he designed, or helped to design, in King Street, Drury Lane, Coronation Square and Legh Road in Knutsford at the turn of the 19th century provide, in the bold informality of their massing and in the free and irregular rhythms of their elevations, a bridge between Gothic revival and the beginnings of the modern movement in architecture. Many of these buildings formed part of the Tatton Estate. In the Knutsford and Alderley Edge area are a few examples of the work of other interesting architects such as Voysey, Percy, Thomas and Hubert Worthington and (at Bexton Croft, Toft Road, Knutsford) Baillie Scott.

The Grosvenors and Chester.

Some Chester architects.

The Tatton Estate and Knutsford.

Bexton Croft, Toft Road, Knutsford — an early house by Baillie Scott, 1895-6.

Comment

Industry.

The legacy from the 19th century which is most obviously at risk is industrial. Old plant and machinery is often superseded and destroyed before its potential historic importance is realised, and the social and environmental difficulties which accompanied the over-fast industrial and urban expansion are still close enough upon us to cause many people to react against all which it produced. Widnes, Warrington and Northwich have great potential interest in this field.

Housing.

The qualities of the better designed and built of the Victorian housing of all types are becoming more widely recognised. Consequently there is now more chance than there was a few years ago that good examples, where they also contain strongly established communities with a clear wish to remain where they live, will be rehabilitated rather than cleared for redevelopment.

Countryside.

The 19th century shares with the 18th century a large contribution to the quality of the farmed landscape and the rural parkland as we know them; this is a heritage lacking adequate financial aid or statutory protection. The concentration on the Grosvenor and Tatton estates in this review should not detract attention from the many important estates such as Crewe Hall, Cholmondeley, Arley, Peckforton, Bolesworth, Capesthorne and others which transformed parts of the countryside.

Communications.

The transport system, railways and 19th century canal works are under no widespread immediate threat. Most of the surviving railways (and probably all those possessing structures or buildings of outstanding interest) appear to have a fairly safe future but their survival is subject to the continuance of government support. The growth of pleasure cruising has saved those canals which have ceased to be used for freight, except where they had decayed before the 1970's.

Craftsmanship and cast iron.

In many parts of Cheshire, especially in and around the town centres, there still remain a host of objects such as lamp-posts, bollards, railings, sign posts and stone pavements which many people already appreciate for their individuality and workmanship, but which are seriously at risk as alterations to roads and open spaces take place.

Equally at risk are the characterful details, such as the shopfronts of Victorian buildings, in shopping and commercial centres.

Offices near Palmyra Square, Warrington, c 1900.

Peckforton estate cottages, Faddiley, mid 19th century.

Late Victorian shop front, Princess Street, Knutsford.

The pace and extent of development in and around our towns since 1914 has been so great and we are still so close upon it that it is not possible in the bounds of this review to attempt a comprehensive assessment.

A few groups of houses, such as those designed by the former Ministry of Works Architects Department at Capenhurst, beside the village green, and some of A. Hepenstall's work of the 1950's at Macclesfield will clearly stand the test of time, as will a small proportion of the larger private houses in Cheshire now standing in mature gardens. One or two groups of public buildings, perhaps most notably the new civic centre at Crewe standing attractively between the earlier municipal buildings and Christchurch — (W.S. Hattrell and Partners, Architects) show quality. The ingeniously designed Grosvenor Shopping Precinct at Chester is likely to remain popular as a lively addition to an old town centre, very well integrated with the Rows, but less harmonious when seem from Pepper Street or the City Walls. (Sir Percy Thomas and Son, Architects). There is skilful architecture and admirable landscaping at Runcorn New Town. (Warrington New Town has not yet had time to show its character). One or two industrial buildings — the Geigy factory at Macclesfield (Martin H. Burckhardt, of Basle, Architect) and the Shell research centre at Thornton, Ellesmere Port (Sir Frederick Gibberd, Architect) are pleasantly designed.

If one can feel hopeful that a small portion of the ordinary building development of the past sixty years may become conservation areas in the future, some aspects of twentieth century communications structures may provide as much interest and pleasure to future generations as the canals and, increasingly, the railways do to us. Just as Cheshire was focal in the networks of those transport systems, so it is now with motorways and main roads. The great steel arch of the new Runcorn — Widnes road bridge (Mott, Hay and Anderson, Engineers) contrasts dramatically with the massive iron and stone of the railway bridge alongside it which is just 100 years older. The distinctive concrete railway bridges over the M62 at Preston Brook and Dutton, cast alongside the railway lines and then rolled into place in a matter of hours so that train services should not be interrupted, are interesting technically and satisfying to look at. (British Railways Engineers). The concrete bridge carrying the Whitefield — Hartford road over the Northwich by-pass (by the former County Surveyor c.1939) is distinguished as an unusually slender, simple and well proportioned design — probably influenced by pre-war German autobahn engineering.

Perhaps the structure of most dramatic impact and lasting interest is in the field of space communications, the Jodrell Bank radio telescope, an instrument with perhaps a limited length of scientific life, but which should in due time be preserved for its historic interest. It remains to be seen whether the current development at the Daresbury nuclear physics laboratory may arouse comparable public interest.

*Hurdsfield Estate, Macclesfield —
council houses of the 1950's
(A. Heppenstall, Borough Architect).*

Jodrell Bank Radio Telescope.

*Tandem Van de Graaff. Nuclear
accelerator Daresbury Nuclear
Physics Laboratory.*

John Douglas

John Douglas led a group of talented architects in late 19th century, Chester.

House in Bath Street, Chester, 1902. Douglas and Minshull.

St. Paul's, Boughton. Douglas took advantage of the site to produce a dramatic composition with "Rhineland" overtones.

Uffington House, Boughton, Chester by EA Ould, a pupil of Douglas.

Werburgh Street, Chester. Douglas's most ambitious range of "black and white" buildings in the old city.

Detail of the King's Coffee House, King Street, Knutsford.

Richard Watts

Watts activated a group of architects and designers who did much under-appreciated work at the turn of the 19th century in Knutsford.

Drury Lane.

Some 20th. Century Buildings and Bridges

The Civic Centre at Crewe. Trees, grass and carefully designed paving among well grouped buildings make an attractive centre. Hattrell and Partners, architects.

These houses at Capenhurst for the Atomic Energy Authority have created a new village green. Architect's Department of the former Ministry of Works.

Precast concrete Railway Bridge, Sutton Weaver. Cast beside the track, the bridge was rolled into position and the track relaid overnight.

Geigy Factory, **Macclesfield.** (MH Burckhardt, Architect).

Laminated Timber Bridge over the river Weaver at Dutton. Engineers to the former Mersey and Weaver River **Board.**

Some Problems in the Conservation of Towns, Buildings and the Countryside

Tackling dereliction: Gamul Terrace, Lower Bridge Street, Chester. Restored by the City of Chester District Council. Donald Insall architect.

Even where hedges are retained modern cutting methods often destroy the saplings which would otherwise grow into future hedgerow trees. Resources are needed urgently to encourage the maintenance and improvement of the face of the farmed landscape.

Dutton Hospital; large, attractive and well built but difficult to convert to a new use. It was quickly vandalised when it closed as a hospital.

Problem of maintenance: pebble dashing rarely solves the defects of rising and penetrating damp. It can make them more difficult to cure.

Pressure for development in town centres has often ignored the quality and restorability of existing buildings.

Problem of quality control in restoration; the use of dense impervious mortar will cause deterioration of the stonework and gives a harsh appearance.

This brief gazetteer identifies some of the places where the imprint of the past and the evolution of the face of Cheshire can most clearly be seen. For more detailed information, primarily on buildings, three books are recommended: for Cheshire south of the Mersey (and for Stockport and the Wirral including Birkenhead and Wallasey) "The buildings of England-Cheshire" by Nikolaus Pevsner and Edward Hubbard (Penguin Books) and for the area north of the Mersey including Widnes and Warrington which is now in Cheshire "The Buildings of England — South Lancashire" by Nikolaus Pevsner (Penguin) and Murray's Guide to Lancashire by Peter Fleetwood-Hesketh.

The places mentioned in the gazetteer are not all named on the maps at the end of the book, but their general location is indicated in the margin by reference to the numbered squares on Map 6.

Places of outstanding general interest are marked with a star, and places of considerable but more specialised interest with the letter S.

An indication of the probable opening times of houses and other places of interest which are open to the public is given wherever possible. At the time of going to press information was available only for 1975. Since opening times may vary from year to year, it is advisable to check before visiting.

F7 **Acton** (near Nantwich) is a picturesque hamlet near the park gates of Dorfold Hall (q.v.). The interesting church contains varied work from 13th to 19th centuries, with good monuments and furnishings inside. Pub, shop, cottages and almshouses are pleasantly grouped amongst trees.

K3 **Adlington Hall** stands in a park west of the Stockport-Macclesfield road. It is partly a late medieval "black-and-white" oak framed Hall, and partly an 18th century brick porticoed house. Friendly and informal in appearance, it

✳ is one of the most attractive houses in Cheshire to visit. (Open summer, Sundays and Bank Holidays; also Saturdays during July and August [in 1975]).

J3/4 **Alderley Edge** is an attractive small town with a 19th century railway-sponsored area of romantically designed houses with mature wooded gardens in the folds of the steep slopes of the Edge. There is a pleasant informal

S "village" shopping centre. Chorley Old Hall, ½ mile west of the centre, easily seen from the A535, is partly 14th century (the oldest Hall in Cheshire) and partly 16th/17th century.

C6 **Aldford**, a wholly 19th century "model" Grosvenor Estate village on an older site at the south eastern gates of Eaton Park, has a good church and stone cottages by John Douglas (1880-1900) and a number of early Victorian cottages.

✳ The earthworks of a motte-and-bailey castle stands north of the churchyard, via a path from behind the church, which also leads to Thomas Telford's fine cast-iron bridge carrying the drive to Eaton Hall across the River Dee.

I7 **Alsager** is largely suburban, much of it late Victorian and Edwardian, originally developed for people travelling by train to work at Stoke-on-Trent; some pleasant parkland adjoins the residential area. There is an 18th century church.

G4 **Anderton**, facing I.C.I.'s Winnington chemical works across the Weaver valley, has the Anderton Lift, built in 1875 to

S raise and lower barges in two counter-balanced suspended docks between the Trent and Mersey Canal and the Weaver Navigation 50 feet below. Originally hydraulically powered, it was converted to electric power at the turn of this century. It was restored in 1974/5 and is now in use for pleasure craft — a very impressive structure.

E5/6 **Arderne Park and Portal Park** form an attractive tract of parkland in rolling countryside immediately north-east of Tarporley (Private).

G3   **The Arley Estate.** The park and gardens (19th century) are good, and the informal Hall (mainly c. 1835) is attractive

*

with a fine, older range of stables and outbuildings. There is a pleasant small estate village at the park gates, and a number of pleasant old estate buildings at Arley Green in the extensive park. Occasional services in chapel. Grounds open to the public during summer (except Mondays, in 1975).

J6   **Astbury** is a very picturesque and interesting small village. The Church (St. Mary) is very fine, outside and in, with many interesting features and furnishings. It has a detached

*

tower with a spire (rare in Cheshire). Church, cottages and pub stand, nicely grouped, around three sides of a small village green on rising ground. Some of the houses are early 19th century estate cottages. The village's full name, seldom used, is Newbold Astbury.

E3/4   **Aston Park** on the east side of the River Weaver south of Runcorn (Humphrey Repton c. 1793) enhances one of the prettiest stretches of the valley. A footpath from Aston to Crowton gives views of park and river and passes under the great stone Dutton Viaduct of the old Grand Junction Railway (George Stephenson and Joseph Locke, engineers). The Hall is demolished.

G9   **Audlem** (as the fine, large church, St. James, largely 14th century, suggests) was an important medieval settlement with pottery kilns. It is now almost a little town, attractive and with varied interest: the church, the 17th century

*

shambles (market house), 17th century old Grammar school (via School Lane south of Stafford Street), 18th/19th century hotels, houses and cottages and the Shropshire Union Canal. Two good oak-framed houses are near the village. Moss Hall, ½ mile north, can be seen from the canal. Highfields is south-east of the village.

H8   **Barthomley,** with narrow, winding lanes is set in pleasant pastoral scenery. The church, St. Bertholine, mostly 15th century, is interesting and stands well on rising ground. The black and white oak-framed pub and cottages are picturesque.

E6   **Beeston.** Not much of a village, but with Cheshire's most

*

impressive castle, and a fanciful 17th century large black-and-white house (now a hotel) south of the village on the A49.

J4   **Birtles** has a good early 19th century stone hall, but the

S

glory of this area is the continuous parkland in the beautiful hilly countryside between Alderley Edge and Macclesfield. Birtles Park adjoins Alderley Park to the west and Henbury Park to the south-east. (Private)

D7   **The Bolesworth Estate** astride the south-western end of the Peckforton Hills has good parkland in pleasant, hilly countryside. Harthill is a well-sited stone-built estate hamlet of the 1840's with a 17th century church and there are numbers of estate farmhouses and cottages (much modified to suit modern needs). Bolesworth Castle (1830) stands well on rising ground in the park (Private).

K3/4   **Bollington,** little more than a large village, lies pleasantly in the Pennine foothills. The central part of this cotton-milling town retains much of its intimate, stone-built Victorian character, as does Kerridge just to the south. The mills in and around the town have industrial archaeological interest.

G5   **Bostock Hall, Park and Village.** North of Middlewich, the good 18th century hall stands in a pleasant park with the informal, rather dispersed estate village of "romantic" 19th century cottages along the road outside the park gates. (Private)

I6   **Brereton Hall,** a fine brick Elizabethan hall, south of Holmes Chapel, (perhaps only a part of the original) stands with the Perpendicular parish church close by in the park. (The Hall is private; access to the church only).

K6   **The Bridestones, Buglawton, Near Congleton.** Remains of

*

a Neolithic or New Stone Age burial chamber.

E7   **Bunbury** has two centres, ½ mile apart. Interest concentrates to the east, where there is a very fine 14th/15th century church (perfectly restored after severe wartime bomb damage). There are pleasantly grouped old cottages on the nearby winding lanes.

A4   **Burton** (near Neston) has a picturesque village street with pleasantly grouped houses and cottages of varied periods. The church is mostly of 1721. Burton Manor (mostly Edwardian) used to belong to the Gladstone family. Liverpool University botanical gardens (open to public) are to the north-west on the Ness road.

  ✲✲   **Canals.** The canals in Cheshire are shown on Map 5 and referred to in Chapters 6 and 7. Little remains of the earliest navigation, the Mersey and Irwell (c. 1700). The St. Helen's Canal (c. 1755) is in semi-ruin and severed in places, but partial restoration is a prospect. The Latchford Canal at Warrington (c. 1820) is closed and unlikely to survive. The Bridgewater Canal, Chester and Ellesmere Port Canal, Llangollen Canal, Macclesfield Canal, Middlewich Branch, Shropshire Union and Trent and Mersey are in full use for pleasure cruising; the Manchester Ship Canal and the Weaver Navigation carry seagoing freighters. Points of interest include the Anderton Lift (q.v.), The Dock Basin at Ellesmere Port (to become a museum), tunnels at Barnton on the Trent and Mersey, lift bridges on the Llangollen Canal (see Wrenbury), early electrically operated swing bridges on the Weaver Navigation and Crosfields' transporter bridge across the River Mersey at Warrington.

I/J4   **Capesthorne Hall** has an expansive park, prominent from the Alderley Edge — Congleton road (A34). The Hall,
   S   appearing to the Elizabethan at first glance, is really mostly the work of A. Salvin (c. 1865). (Open several days each week during summer months, in 1975).

D7/8   **The Carden Estate.** Rolling parkland and woodland just south-west of the Peckforton/Bickerton Hills. There are a number of 19th century farms and cottages and Stretton Mill (in course of restoration as a museum by Cheshire County Council in 1975), is of special interest, with 18th century machinery in an older building.

C5   **Chester.** The view expressed in The Buildings of England (Cheshire, N. Pevsner and E. Hubbard) that "Chester is not
  ✲✲   a medieval, it is a Victorian city" does not do the place justice. The character and quality of the many "romantic" Victorian buildings in the town centre (Eastgate Street, Northgate Street and St. Werburgh Street) and in Bath Street and Grosvenor Park Road south of Foregate Street are exceptional, but for many visitors the special interest of the city will lie in the length of history which its form, location and buildings reflect.

Roman remains include the main street pattern of the legionary fortress (Bridge St, Eastgate Street, Watergate Street and, approximately, Northgate Street), the military amphitheatre, fragments of the city walls and much more (see Grosvenor Museum). Medieval remains include the fine Norman/Transitional (11th-13th century) church of St. John the Baptist, the Cathedral and Abbey remains (work from 11th-20th century), St. Mary-on-the-Hill (Decorated and Perpendicular — now deconsecrated) and other less distinguished churches, the city walls and Castle, the Old Dee Bridge (14th century, altered), the layout (but only fragments of buildings) of the unique Rows — the two-level shopping galleries in Eastgate Street, Bridge Street, Watergate Street and Northgate Street. Unfortunately nothing remains of the medieval port — or of the famous Mill of Dee.

A number of major oak-framed town houses of the 17th century suggest growing prosperity, except during the Civil War — notably the Bear and Billet, the Old King's Head and the Falcon in Lower Bridge Street and Bishops Lloyd's House and the Stanley Palace in Watergate Street, and, in brick, Gamul House, Lower Bridge Street.

Sustained prosperity during the 18th century brought some good terraces and squares of Georgian urban houses — including Abbey Square, Abbey Street and Abbey Green north of the Cathedral, King Street west of Northgate Street, Stanley Place north of Lower Watergate Street and Nicholas Street (west side) now on the inner ring road and traffic-filled. The main shopping streets retain a good number of Georgian frontages. Chester's most distinguished Georgian buildings are by Thomas Harrison (1744-1829) — the public buildings around the Castle Square off Grosvenor Street, the noble Grosvenor Bridge across the Dee and the City Club on Northgate Street just by St. Peter's church.

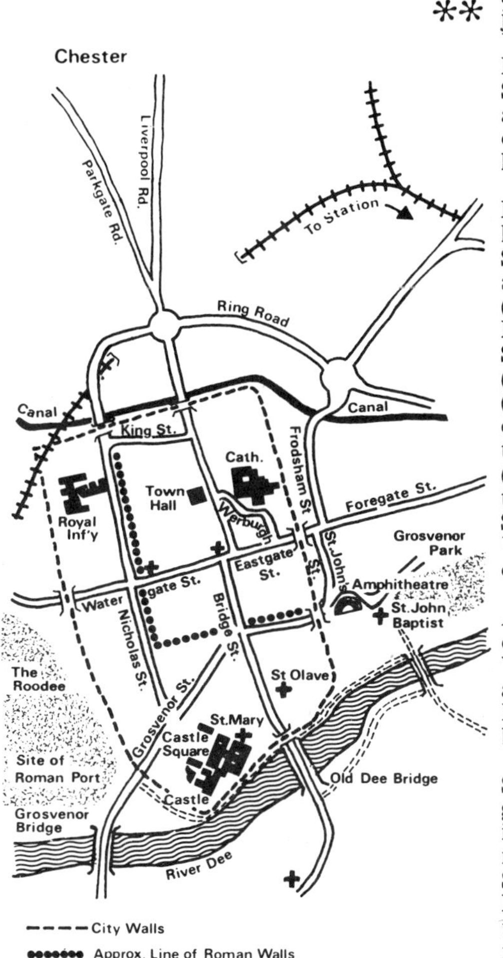

Also worth seeing are the Chester Canal ladder of locks north-west of the Northgate, the Bluecoat school (outside the Northgate), the Royal Infirmary (north of the Watergate) and the old Bishop's Palace (YMCA) overlooking the Dee by St. John's church. Nearby is the beautiful 19th century Grosvenor Park.

Apart from the Victorian rebuilding in and near the town centre already referred to, the railway station (F. Thompson 1847) and the square in front of it and the town hall (W.H. Lynn, 1864) are prominent amongst a number of good individual buildings. St. Paul's church, Boughton, by John Douglas, is of interest, especially internally and as seen from the river.

The 20th century has brought one or two good buildings (some in the old tradition) in St. Werburgh Street and Foregate Street, and the Grosvenor precinct, a major extension to the shopping centre which links Eastgate Street, Bridge Street, Pepper Street and the City Walls.

E8
***** **The Cholmondeley Estate** has a very good park around Cholmondeley Castle — early Gothic Revival, partly by Sir Robert Smirke (1817). A number of good 19th century farms and other buildings stand in and around the park, and an interesting partly 17th century chapel (public services). There are good 19th century ornamental gardens. Grounds open very occasionally, as advertised locally.

D5 **Christleton**, burned by the Royalist defenders of Chester during the Civil War, has attractive stone-walled lanes and a number of good 17th and 18th century houses. The church is mostly of 1875 by William Butterfield.

G6 **Church Minshull**, in a pleasant reach of the Weaver Valley, has a Queen Anne brick church, one or two old houses and a few nicely grouped estate cottages.

C7 **Churton** has pleasant winding stone-walled lanes with a number of attractive 17th, 18th and 19th century houses, but no church. Churton Hall, 17th century, is oak-framed.

D7 **Coddington** is attractively grouped in pleasant pastoral landscape, untouched by new development. The artificial mound in the centre of the village is an Ancient Monument, thought to be a Saxon burial mound.

F9
***** **Combermere Abbey.** The interesting Hall is on the site of the Benedictine Abbey, of which little remains above ground. The park with the Mere fringed with woodland, lies in very pleasant rolling countryside. The Hall was built or rebuilt by stages from the 16th to the 19th century. (Private)

J6 **Congleton** does not immediately show its interest. Much of the medieval street pattern survives, and something of the 18th century development generated by the early silk industry. There are probably a number of Tudor and Jacobean buildings behind 18th and 19th century facades. Moody Street has good Georgian houses, with the Church of St. Peter (1740) nearby. There are some survivals of 18th century mills (Mill Street) and houses (West Street).

G/H7 **Crewe** was created by the 19th century Grand Junction Railway Company. Little of the original railway town remains: the station (in part), railway offices at Chester Bridge, Christ Church, St. Paul's, Hightown and St. Barnabas, West Street (all Railway Co. churches), the Municipal Offices, Earle Street (J.T. Hare 1902), Crewe Theatre (also J.T. Hare 1887) with a distinguished, lively neo-baroque auditorium in an unprepossessing exterior; and a very good park (Queen's Park, Victoria Avenue, 1887). Very little of the original railway housing survives. There is a good modern civic centre (W.S. Hattrell and Partners) between Earle Street and Christ Church.

H7
***** **Crewe Hall and Estate.** The Jacobean Hall, with extensive alteration internally (by E.M. Barry, 1868) is very fine, and set in a beautiful, mature park. There are some good mid-Victorian estate cottages at the edge of the park, especially at its south-west corner. The park is broad and attractive, designed by Humphrey Repton. (Private; leased from the Duchy of Lancaster by the Wellcome Foundation).

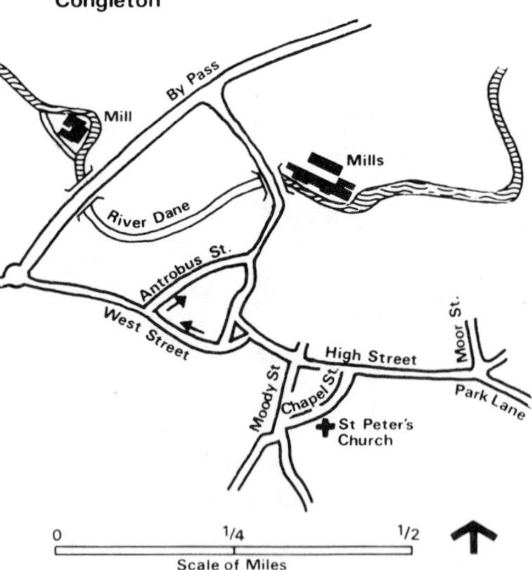

Congleton

F3   **Daresbury** is an attractive village, mostly 19th century, where Lewis Carrol spent part of his boyhood; ½ mile north is the Daresbury nuclear research laboratory.

E4/5   **Delamere Forest**, a medieval Royal Forest, used to stretch from Frodsham to Nantwich. Only a few square miles remain, in pleasant undulating countryside between Frodsham and Helsby, managed by the Forestry Commission and largely planted with conifers. There is a forestry museum at Delamere, near the railway station, and many signposted forest walks.
✳

L2   **Disley**, almost a small town, with a few pleasant old buildings, stands near the main gates of Lyme Park (q.v.).

H8/9   **Doddington Park** was landscaped by Capability Brown. The fine Hall (Samuel Wyatt, 1777) stands beyond a broad mere (club sailing). The park contains a well-preserved 14th century fortified tower (Doddington Castle), visible from the A51, 6 miles south-east of Nantwich. (Private)
✳

B6   **Dodleston** is partly a Grosvenor Estate village. The church (St. Mary, 1870) is largely by John Douglas. Just south of the churchyard are remains of a motte-and-bailey castle.

F/G 7/8   **Dorfold Hall**, on the Chester road 1 mile from Nantwich, has an exceptionally fine brick Jacobean Hall in a good park, with the interesting, small old village of Acton at the park gates. (Private)
✳

F6   **Eaton** (near Tarporley) has a large number of oak-framed cottages, mostly 17th century (?), attractively grouped along narrow, winding village lanes. The church, St. Thomas, 1896, has no special interest.

C6   **Eaton Hall and Park.** See Grosvenor Estate.

C6   **Eccleston** is probably the best of a good set of 19th century Grosvenor Estate villages. It stands at the gates of Eaton Park by the west bank of the Dee. The church (St. Mary, 1899) is one of G.F. Bodley's best designs. Most of the houses and cottages in the village are by John Douglas, full of inventive variety, as is the school. There is a beautiful (but rather neglected) riverside footpath upstream to the Iron Bridge and Aldford.
S

E5   **Eddisbury Camp, Delamere.** Early Iron Age hillfort sacked by the Romans and later re-occupied as a Saxon burgh. On private land but visible from the Sandstone Trail.
✳

C4   **Ellesmere Port** has grown in three stages: as the Mersey entrance to the Ellesmere Canal in 1795, Manchester Ship Canal and docks, 1895, and Ship Canal-served oil and chemical industries in the mid 20th century, plus a General Motors car factory. The Ellesmere Canal dock basin and buildings are interesting (now being converted to form an Inland Waterway Museum) and the oil refineries are impressive, if ugly.

C7   **Farndon** is a large Deeside village with a fine medieval sandstone bridge. St. Chad's church was rebuilt in 1658 after severe damage during the Civil War. The curving main street and the lanes around the church are lined with pleasant groups of old houses. On the north edge of its village is the Barnston Obelisk (1858). Holt, across the Dee in Wales, has remains of a castle (on private land).
✳

K3   **Foxtwist Moated Site 2 Miles North of Prestbury.** Impressive medieval moated enclosure south-east of Woodside Farm. Probable site of the 14th century hall of Robert de Foxtwist. (Private land)

E 3/4 **Frodsham** is, in all but name, a little town. The spacious
tree-lined Main Street is flanked by a large number of good
★ buildings, mostly 18th and early 19th century, but one or
two, including the Bear's Paw inn, 17th century. The
church (St. Laurence) standing on the hillside above the
village, incorporates building work or furnishings from the
11th to 19th century.

The navigable River Weaver flows just east of the village,
with 19th century waterside warehouses, a fine stone and
cast-iron railway viaduct, a swing bridge for the main road
and a heavy, broad concrete viaduct for the M56 motorway.

Frodsham is at the north end of the mid-Cheshire Ridge,
attractive countryside containing a number of prehistoric
sites, and is near to Delamere Forest.

K5 **Gawsworth** is of exceptional interest, but a curious village
devoid of cottages and small houses. It stands in the
★★ parkland of Gawsworth Hall and New Hall (q.v.). The
unusual, finely-set church (St. James) contains interesting
stained glass, furnishings and monuments. The Old Rectory
is a large 15th century oak-framed house. An avenue leads
from the church to the main Congleton road. Samuel
Johnson, England's last licensed Court Jester (18th
century) is buried here in "Maggotty Johnson's Wood"
(monument).

K5 **Gawsworth Hall and New Hall.** The two Halls stand in
parkland which also encompasses the old part of the village.
★★ The Old Hall is one of Cheshire's best "black-and-white"
oak-framed houses. Opposite it, with fish-ponds between,
is the "Queen Anne" New Hall (1707). The Halls,
dependent buildings, fish ponds, gardens, park and
village offer a great variety of beauty and historic interest.
(New Hall private; Old Hall, home of the antiquary and
architectural historian, Mr. Raymond Richards, is open
daily during summer months [in 1975]). The New Hall
was a home of the Lord Mohun who figures in Thackeray's
"Henry Esmond".

F/G 2 **Grappenhall** is attractive. The village street is cobbled, the
church (St. Wilfred) is of many periods but mainly 16th
century, and (good) 19th century. There are two or three
old houses, a well-sited pub and a lot of mature trees. The
street crosses the Bridgewater Canal near the eastern end of
the old village.

D5 **Great Barrow** is a pleasant, leafy village on a low hillock
south of the Mersey valley, with buildings informally
grouped along a network of village lanes. St. Bartholomew
is a 17th and 18th century church restored by John Douglas.
There is a ruinous water mill.

G 3/4 **Great Budworth** is a most interesting and beautiful village,
on a low hill overlooking Budworth Mere and the Weaver
★★ Valley. St. Mary's Church is large and fine, mostly 15th/
16th century. The narrow winding village street turns
sharply and opens into a little square in front of the church.
The old school (16th/17th century) stands in the
churchyard. Almost all the buildings (17th to 20th
century) along the village street and around the church
add pleasantly to the scene. They are grouped informally
and unpretentious, including a number of old oak-framed
cottages. The George and Dragon, opposite the church,
is by John Douglas.

I5 **Goostrey** is 1 mile south of the Jodrell Bank radio
telescope.

B6, C6/7 **The Grosvenor Estate**, centering on Eaton Hall, by the
Dee near Eccleston is a large, mainly 19th century estate,
★★ with many features of interest and beauty. Alfred
Waterhouse's fine chapel and stables (1875) survive next
to the new Hall (1972). The good extensive park, with
fine gardens by Sir Edwin Lutyens and Elizabeth Jekyll,
in front of the Hall, is surrounded by some 15 square miles
of estate farmland with several "model" villages and hamlets
(Aldford, Bruera, part of Dodleston, Eccleston, Poulton,
Pulford, Saighton and Waverton), q.v. The villages,
farmland and park contain many buildings by John Douglas
and his colleagues. (Riverside footpath through park from
Eccleston to Aldford. Gardens, chapel and stables
occasionally open on summer Sundays, as advertised.)

D3   **Hale** (west of Widnes) is a pleasant village, with parkland
S   adjoining (including a rare 17th century duck decoy, south
of the Widnes road), near to the northern shore of the
Mersey estuary (lighthouse). The church (St. Mary) is
mostly 18th century. The Manor House (originally the
parsonage) has a very attractive Queen Anne classical front
(c. 1710). There are a few old cottages and some 19th
century estate cottages on the village street (a cul-de-sac,
leading to Hale Head on the Mersey shore).

D7   **Harthill** See Bolesworth Estate.

C6   **Heronbridge Roman Site, Claverton.** An extensive site on
both sides of the Roman Watling Street where it passes
close to the River Dee. The site was fortified in post-Roman
times and earthworks can be seen between the present road
and the river. (Private land)

E5   **High Billinge Tumulus, Utkinton,** a round burial mound,
probably of the Bronze Age. Planted with a very prominent
stand of trees on private land, but visible from the
Sandstone Trail.

H3   **High Legh** on the A50 between Warrington and Knutsford
has pleasant parkland and a 19th century estate hamlet in a
well-wooded setting.

H/I5   **Holmes Chapel** is a large village with much modern
residential development. There is a pleasant, short, village
street with some 18th century buildings. St. Luke's church,
beside a little square on the street, is interesting; a large
15th century oak-framed church cased in brick during the
18th century.

D4   **Ince,** just east of Ellesmere Port, between oil refineries,
✳   power station and fertiliser factory, is of unexpected
interest. It has substantial remains of a medieval grange
of St. Werburgh's Abbey, Chester. St. James' Church,
on a little knoll, has 14th, 15th, 17th and 19th century
work and there is some Georgian estate housing.

I4/5   **Jodrell Bank Radio Telescope** is, of course, primarily for
✳   astronomical use, but it has also become famous for its part
in tracking American and Russian space probes. Open to
the public winter week-ends (2-5 pm) and every day in
summer from Easter to the end of October (2-6 pm).

H4   **Lower Peover** is a very attractive hamlet with school, a pub
✳   (which caters) and cottages around the churchyard of
St. Oswald. The church is of special interest — a 13th or
14th century oak-framed building except for the later
tower, which is of stone.

G2   **Lymm,** scarcely more than a village, has few buildings of
S   distinction but a most attractive overall character with
countryside and parkland penetrating to the town centre.
The main street is informal and pretty, with the old mill
pool in a little wooded valley adjoining it. There are a
number of pleasant 17th, 18th and 19th century buildings
and the Bridgewater canal skirts the north of the shopping
centre.

K/L3   **Lyme Hall and Lyme Park.** Lyme Hall is one of the finest
and largest country houses in Cheshire, with an interesting
✳✳   sequence of work from 1550 to 1820. Notable are the
Elizabethan wing and the work (c. 1720) by Giacomo
Leoni. The large park and woodlands in the folds of the
Pennine foothills are very attractive. (The Hall was open
in 1975 March-October except Mondays; the park all year.
National Trust property managed by Stockport District
Council).

K4   **Kerridge,** partly a suburb of Bollington, is all stone-built
S   and finely situated on the wooded slopes of Kerridge ridge,
a steep and beautiful little outlyer of the Pennines, capped
with a curious "folly" called White Nancy.

L3   **Kettleshulme** is a stone-built Pennine village. In the valley
below is Lumbhole water-mill, in which a steam beam-
engine survives. It was used when the mill needed more
power than the water-wheel could supply.

H3 **Knutsford** has three main attractions: uniquely (for
✳ Cheshire) it retains the character of a Georgian country
town, it adjoins the interesting and very popular Tatton
Park (q.v.) and it was the scene of operations of a talented
group of architects and designers at the turn of the 19th
century. The Parish Church (St. John Baptist, 1741), the
classical Sessions House (G. Moneypenny [?] 1815) and
the old Town Hall (Alfred Waterhouse, 1870) are on Toft
Road; the railway station and the 17th century Unitarian
chapel on Adams Hill; good Georgian buildings (inc.
Royal George Hotel) and R.H. Watt's King's Coffee House
(1907) are on King Street, a good romantic terrace of
buildings on Drury Lane (off north end of King Street)
by Watt and his associates, some good Georgian and 19th
century buildings on Princess Street, and characterful large
houses by Watt, Walter Aston, Harry Fairhurst, John
Brooke, Paul Ogden, Sir Hubert Worthington and Baille
Scott on Legh Road, Leycester Road, Chelford Road and
Toft Road. Mrs. Gaskell caught the social character of mid-
Victorian Knutsford in her book "Cranford".

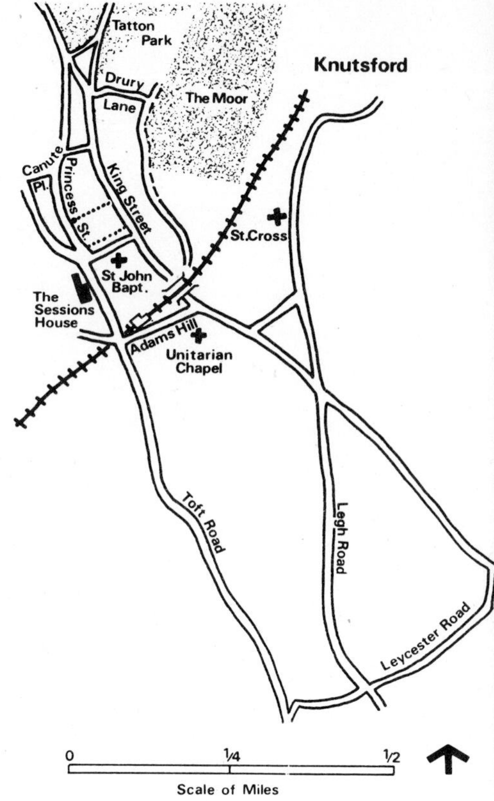

K4 **Macclesfield**, finely set with the town centre on a steep
knoll looking across the narrow Bollin valley to the
Pennines, does not at first sight do justice to its historic
S interest. St. Michael's church alone remains from the
Middle Ages, but the streets and stepped walks around it
give some feel of the character of a medieval town. The
small, hand-worked bottle-shaped coal pits east of the
Bollin and the 17th century industries of the town have
left few traces. Charles Roe brought a major change in
1743 when he opened his first silk mill. Frost's Mill,
Mill Green and the Card Factory, Chester Road, survive
from the 18th century. There are a number of terraces of
handloom weavers' cottages west and south of the town
centre. West of London Road and south of Park Street is
an area built for an early 19th century community of
textile workers: dwellings, including weavers' cottages,
chapels, schools and shops. Charles Roe lived at a good
Queen Anne house (62, Chestergate).

Other buildings worth seeing include St. Alban's R.C.
church, Chester Road (A.W.N. Pugin, 1839), the
Victorian militia barracks to the south, Christ Church,
Catherine Street, 1775, the huge Sunday School, Roe
Street (1813), a number of buildings in Park Green, the
Town Hall, Market Place (1823, Francis Goodwin),
buildings in Market Place and Brunswick Hill, Jordangate
House (1728), Cumberland House and the Macclesfield
Arms Hotel (1811) in Jordangate, a house (now offices)
on the N. side of King Edward Street and Arighi Bianchi's
cast-iron fronted furniture showroom (1882) in
Commercial Road east of the railway.

The 19th century parks, especially West Park and Victoria
Park, are good. The modern Sparrow Park, behind the
Town Hall, offers fine views.

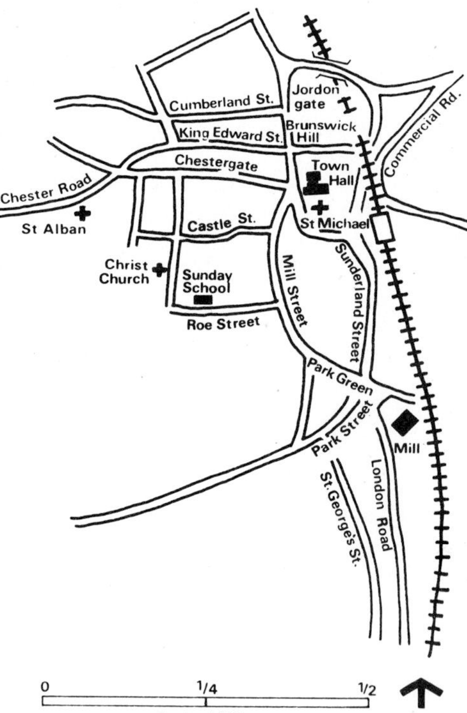

D8 **Malpas**, of outstanding interest, is almost a small town.
The village streets curve round the south and east side of
✳✳ the motte-and-bailey castle (north-east of the churchyard).
The church (St. Oswald) is large and fine, 14th — 16th
century, with very interesting furnishings and monuments.
There is a 17th century tithebarn, an 18th century
schoolhouse and a number of good, very pleasantly
grouped, houses and shops. The village stands on a knoll,
crowned by the church with its tower.

E9 **Marbury** (near Malpas) is pleasantly set between two meres,
with some oak-framed houses around a beautifully situated
Perpendicular (15th century) church, with later alterations.

J5 **Marton** has an interesting 14th century oak-framed church
(on the A34).

H5/6 **Middlewich** has a long history as a salt-producing town,
but few remains survive. There was a Romano-British
settlement (Salinae), not yet fully investigated. The fine,
large church (St. Michael) is dominant, mostly 15th/16th
century, but with traces of Norman work. There are a few
pleasant 18th and 19th century houses in the central area,
and the Trent and Mersey canal passes close to the church,
with a branch to the Shropshire Union canal joining it to
the south.

I3 **Mobberley** is a rather straggling village, but with 14th – 16th century church and a number of houses of interest, from 17th to early 20th century.

E/F 2/3 **Moore** has a picturesque village street with a number of pleasant 17th, 18th and 19th century buildings. The Bridgewater Canal runs through the village.

J6/7 **Moreton Hall, Great** (Private) is a good castellated "gothic" Hall by Edward Blore (1841) with parkland which extends
✶✶ to **Little Moreton Hall (Moreton Old Hall)** the best known oak-framed black-and-white house in Cheshire. It is picturesquely moated. The oldest part of the Hall is the Great Hall (late 15th century); the later parts are mostly 16th century. (Open, afternoons, except Tuesdays, March – End of October, National Trust).

J3 **Mottram Hall and Old Hall** are interesting buildings with pleasant parkland in good, rolling scenery between Wilmslow and Prestbury (Private).

J7 **Mow Cop**, a former mining village, and the birthplace of
S primitive methodism, caps a 1,000 ft hill, with a very early mock gothic castle (1754; National Trust Property).

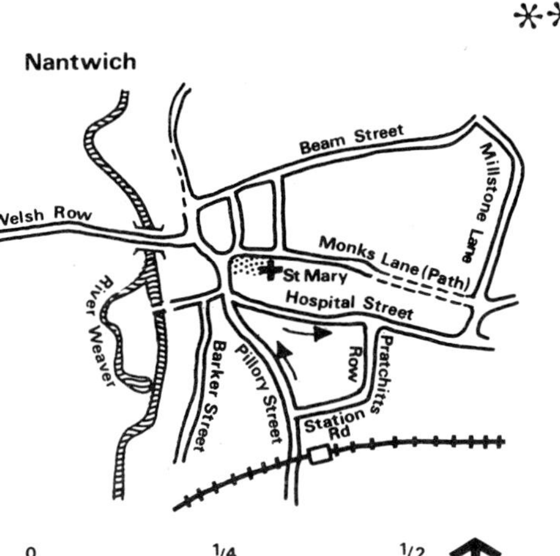

G7/8 **Nantwich** is of outstanding interest. It dominated Cheshire's medieval and Jacobean salt trade and was a centre of tanning
✶✶ and, apparently, pottery during the Middle Ages. It had a castle (the site is not yet determined for certain) and it has one of Cheshire's most beautiful churches (St. Mary, mostly 14th century, in an attractive churchyard surrounded by buildings of interest). A fire destroyed most of the town in 1583, leaving one very interesting earlier oak-framed house of 1577 (Churche's Mansion, now a restaurant, well restored, in Hospital Street). The Crown Hotel (High Street) and Sweetbriar Hall (Hospital Street) stand out amongst a number of good 17th century oak-framed buildings. Interesting, attractive buildings of the 17th, 18th and 19th centuries abound in Welsh Row, High Street, Barker Street, Pillory Street, Hospital Street and Monks Lane. At the east end of Beam Street are the 17th century Wright's and 18th century Crewe's Almshouses, recently restored and radically improved. The River Weaver flows immediately west of the town centre (good classical bridge, High Street) and the Shropshire Union Canal skirts the town (aqueduct by Thomas Telford, Chester Road).

A4 **Neston**, with Parkgate was a main 18th century port for
S Ireland and, until the 1820's the biggest town in the Wirral. It is now largely a residential town for people who work elsewhere. Parkgate has a good former sea-front, the Parade, now facing the salt-marshes of the silted-up estuary, with a fair number of Georgian buildings. There are some good detached Georgian houses nearer the centre of Neston on Parkgate Road.

J4 **Nether Alderley** stands in beautiful parkland, and has several interesting buildings. The 17th century water mill
✶ (with 19th century machinery) is restored and owned by the National Trust, open Wednesday and Sunday 2 - 5 pm in summer). Beside the large, tree-fringed mill-pool is the fine 16th century Old Hall. The good Perpendicular church has interesting features inside. In the churchyard is the former school (1693). The 17th century Eagle and Child Cottage was a staging-house during the coaching age.

G4 **Northwich** was a Roman salt town (Condate) and a major medieval centre attested by the size of its good 14th – 16th century church (St. Helens). Now primarily a salt and chemical industry town, Northwich had until recently ship-building yards, launching their products abeam into the narrow but navigable River Weaver. Much of the town's interest is for the waterway enthusiast and the industrial archaeologist. The lower swing bridge over the Weaver is thought to be the earliest electrically operated one in the world. There are some attractive waterway buildings and a long stone and cast-iron railway viaduct (1869). Many of the black-and-white buildings were designed to be lifted by special jacks in case of salt subsidence, which used to be common in Northwich.

E7 **The Peckforton Estate.** Peckforton Castle (A. Salvin,
✳ c. 1845) stands in heavily wooded parkland on the steep
ridge of the Peckforton Hills, a spectacular Victorian
composition. Peckforton village picturesquely combines
old oak-framed cottages and 19th century estate cottages.
The great extent of the 19th century estate's farmland can
be traced from the style of farmhouses and cottages; their
ornamental iron casements often have hexagonal panes.
(Private; The "Sandstone Trail", a public footpath, gives
views of park and, in the distance, the Castle.)

I3 **Peover Hall, Radbroke Hall and Toft Hall** have extensive
H/I 4 parkland south of Knutsford. Peover Hall is part of a large
15th century brick house, picturesque. Toft Hall may be
originally 17th century, but with later alterations. Peover
Hall is normally open on Mondays during summer months.
Stables only on Thursdays during summer.

K3 **Pott Shrigley** is an attractive hamlet in a very beautiful
Pennine-foothill setting. St. Christopher's church is mainly
15th/16th century, standing against a background of
wooded hills.

K3 **Poynton** is a large 19th century red-brick colliery village.
The colliery closed (about 1950) and the village is
increasingly the home of people who work in the
Manchester conurbation. St. George's is an impressive
steepled mid-19th century church at the village centre.

K3/4 **Prestbury** has a large suburban fringe which almost joins it
✳ to Macclesfield, but it retains a very interesting and
attractive old centre. The churchyard contains a largish
parish church (St. Peter) — the usual Cheshire mixture
with 13th — 15th century predominating, restored and
altered in the 18th and 19th centuries. There is a separate
restored Norman chapel with a good west front (Norman
work is rare in Cheshire village churches). The village street
is mainly Georgian, with one or two interesting earlier
buildings (especially the oak-framed house, now the
National Westminster Bank, 16th century). Recent minor
alterations to shops and houses have rather damaged the
unity and quality of detail in the village street.

The River Bollin flows past the churchyard, and there is
good, hilly parkland immediately west of the village.

B6/7 **Pulford** is a village in the Grosvenor Estate (q.v.). The
church (1881, by John Douglas) stands immediately north
of the earthworks of a motte-and-bailey castle. There are
typical Grosvenor cottages and pub, in a leafy landscape.

K/L 4 **Rainow** is attractive for its setting in the steep Pennine
foothills and for the well-grouped stone cottages in the old
part of the village. Immediately south is a new nicely
landscaped reservoir.

I7 **Rode Hall** built and enlarged in several stages through the
18th and early 19th centuries stands in a large, well-planted
park immediately south-west of Little Moreton Hall.
(Private)

H3 **Rostherne.** See Tatton Park.

D/E 3 **Runcorn** has a good deal of varied interest which has to be
S looked for. Halton, Weston and Higher Runcorn are old villages dating from before Runcorn began to grow with canal, shipping and chemical industries in the 19th century.
✳ Norton Priory is of outstanding interest, recently excavated (open during summer months, afternoons except Mondays). Halton village has its castle and a number of interesting 17th, 18th and 19th century buildings on Main Street and Castle Street. The Bridgewater Canal came down to the Mersey at Runcorn. (Bridgewater House, occasional residence of the canal-building Duke and Dukesfield, a 19th century housing development for canal workers, are nearby.) There are still a few attractive terraces of 18th and 19th century houses near the water-front east of the road viaduct, and a good parish church (All Saints, 1847, by A. Salvin). The railway viaduct, stone and cast iron, by W. Baker, 1864, and the road bridge over the Mersey estuary (Mott, Hay and Anderson, 1957) are spectacular. Runcorn New Town has interesting housing and a distinctive main shopping centre.

C/D 6 **Saighton.** The gatehouse survives of Saighton Grange, a
✳ principal residence of the abbots of St. Werburgh's Abbey, Chester (1490). It is attached to a large Victorian house, designed to harmonise. Saighton is a Grosvenor Estate village, with cottages by John Douglas. The church (St. Mary, Norman) is at Bruera, 1 mile south.

H6 **Sandbach** has an attractive and interesting centre, but
S straggling ribbons of undistinguished buildings along the Middlewich and Crewe roads. There is an extremely popular Thursday market. The cobbled Market Place contains two large Saxon crosses. Numbers of pleasantly grouped, interesting buildings (from 17th to 19th century) flank the Market Place and nearby streets and lanes. The church (St. Mary) was heavily restored by George Gilbert Scott (1847). Good buildings include the Old Vicarage Hotel, 1656, the Old Town Hall (by T. Bower of Nantwich, 1889) and adjoining buildings, romantically grouped, which have a lot of character.

C8 **Shocklach,** a dispersed village, has a small, largely Norman church (rare for Cheshire) and the earthworks of a motte-and-bailey castle (with another, at Castleton, nearby).

B4 **Shotwick,** secluded, at the end of a narrow cul-de-sac lane, has much historic interest. It had a medieval harbour (the remains have yet to be searched for). St. Michael's church shows work of all periods, from late Norman to 18th century. Shotwick Hall is a warm, informal 17th century brick house and there are several other attractive houses and cottages, pleasantly grouped amongst trees. There is a moat just east of the village. Shotwick Castle site with earthworks remaining, is 1½ miles south-east of the village.

K3 **Shrigley Hall** between Bollington and Poynton is a good Regency house in exceptionally attractive parkland on the Pennine foothills. (Private; now the Salesian College of St. John Bosco.)

J3 **Styal** is an exceptionally complete and interesting 18th century cotton milling village, in a beautiful parkland
✳-✳ setting on the northern shoulder of the Bollin valley. Samuel Greg came from Belfast to build the mill (Quarry Bank) in 1784. He housed his employees (including orphan [?] apprentices) and provided chapel and school. Village and Mill are National Trust property, with adjacent woodland and riverside walks.

I5 **Swettenham Hall** (17th century with 18th century "gothick" remodelling) and the adjoining Davenport House and Somerford Hall stand in scenically attractive parkland in the Dane Valley. Swettenham is a picturesque secluded estate hamlet (unsuited to motor traffic). (Private)

H4 **Tabley Park.** The well-planted park (2 miles west of
✳ Knutsford) contains Tabley House, very fine, by John Carr of York (1761). There is a mere (painted by J.M.W. Turner), an interesting chapel and remains of the old hall. (Private).

E6 * **Tarporley**, almost a little town, has a good Georgian High Street, including a pleasant coaching house, the Swan. The church is mostly Victorian restoration, but the churchyard contains an old school building (now a recreation hall), 1636. Undulating, well-planted parkland adjoins the north-east side of the village. There are some good views of Beeston Castle and the Peckforton Hills.

D7 **Tattenhall**, is a large village, partly influenced by the nearby Bolesworth Estate (Rose Corner, 1927, by Clough Williams Ellis and Rosemary Row opposite). The village street is long, winding and lined by attractively varied, informally grouped buildings with one or two pleasant side lanes. The church (St. Albans) is largely by John Douglas, 1869. There is an interesting, well-designed modern school, with a village green created around it (J. Whittle, County Architect).

H2/3 **I3** ** **Tatton Park** has great interest and variety. The Hall (Samuel & Lewis Wyatt, c. 1788) stands in a large park landscaped by Humphrey Repton, and with extensive estate farmland beyond. There is a fine Mere (club sailing), an interesting Old Hall (to be restored) and fine 19th century gardens. The Hall contains a good collection of pictures and there is much of interest preserved from the 19th century estate. Rostherne, north of the park, is partly an estate village, picturesque and set in pleasant landscape (with very good views from the churchyard). (Tatton Park is a National Trust property, managed by Cheshire County Council). (House open during summer, park all year to pedestrians, except Mondays).

H3 **Tatton Park, Deserted Medieval Village**. Mounds and hollows representing the house plots, crofts and lanes of a deserted village immediately north-east of Tatton Old Hall (National Trust land).

F/G5 **S** **Vale Royal** is the site of a great Cistercian Abbey on the west bank of the Weaver (between Northwich and Winsford) where the river, in a steep, wooded valley, flows between low hills. There is a good park in pleasant rolling scenery and a small, prettily set parkgate village, Whitegate. The large Hall (17th — 19th centuries) is interesting but not outstanding. Few remains are visible of the Abbey. (Private, but with a public footpath along the riverside.)

F2 **S** **Warrington** is an interesting old town, not well enough appreciated. There is nothing to be seen on site of the Romano-British industrial settlement at Wilderspool (see Warrington Museum for remains). There is little above ground from the Middle Ages except the fine church of St. Elphin with some 14th century work, but mostly dating from the 19th century (the steeple and much rebuilding, well designed by F. and H. Francis, 1859), but there is considerable potential interest for the archaeologist below ground in Warrington. Part of Bewsey Old Hall (16th — 19th century) remains north-west from the town centre, across the St. Helens canal.

For many visitors the remains from the 18th and 19th centuries will be of most immediate interest. The finest building is Bank Hall in Sankey Street (now the Town Hall) by James Gibbs, 1750. It stands, a distinguished house, in a small public park with good mid 19th century iron railings and gates to Sankey Street. There are some good Georgian town houses in Sankey Street, and Holy Trinity church, 1760, with a later tower and cupola. Elsewhere are scattered 18th and 19th century houses and shops of some interest, but the late 19th century offers a planned development, now somewhat depleted but still showing buildings and layout of good quality, at Palmyra Square and adjoining streets.

The Old Academy at Bridgefoot (disused and under threat of demolition) is of historic as well as architectural interest. It was an important centre of 18th century scientific education.

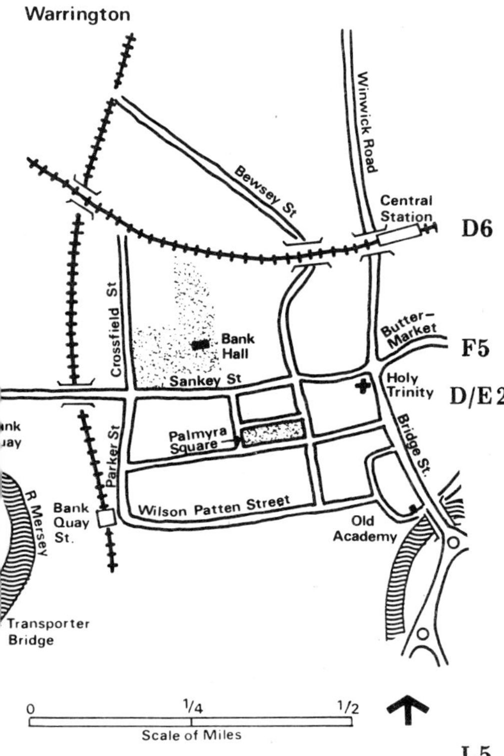

Warrington has always been a centre of communications. The interesting waterways, except for the Bridgewater Canal and the Manchester Ship Canal, are in decay — the St. Helens canal (1755), fragments of the Mersey and Irwell Navigation (c. 1700) and the Latchford canal (c. 1820). Crosfield's transporter bridge (200 yards south-west of Bank Quay Station) across the navigable Mersey is now disused. Bank Quay is the site of Joseph Crosfield's early soapworks (1814), of some interest in the history of our chemical industries.

D6   **Waverton,** is a Grosvenor Estate (q.v.) hamlet. The old school is by John Douglas, who also much restored the church. The hamlet is nicely grouped around the church, prominent in a level landscape, alongside the Chester canal.

F5   **Whitegate.** See Vale Royal (estate).

D/E2   **Widnes** is primarily of interest to the industrial archaeologist, a site of major developments in England's 19th century chemical industry. It has the world's earliest railway company operated dock which, together with remains of Hutchinson's first Leblanc Process soda works, is being preserved at Spike Island. Only the ticket-office and landing-stage·of the former transporter bridge to Runcorn remains, just east of the new road bridge. The water-front has a deserted promenade with good views across the Mersey estuary, and of the great road and railway bridges. A good Edwardian church (St. Mary, by Austin and Paley), the potentially very attractive Mersey Hotel and some well-tended terraces of Victorian housing stand around the promenade. The area is called West Bank.

L5   **Wildboarclough** is a small village, beautifully set in a steep Pennine valley, surrounded by woodland belts and the landscaped park of Crag Hall (classical early 19th century).

J3   **Wilmslow** has a thriving little town centre, a 15th — 16th century church, pleasantly set in the wooded valley of the River Bollin north of the shopping centre, a few scattered good buildings (from the 17th to the 20th century) including some comfortable 19th century houses for Manchester businessmen.

L5   **Wincle** is a small Pennine stone-built village.

G4   **Winnington,** site of John Brunner and Ludwig Mond's great **S** 19th century leap forward in heavy chemicals technology, now accommodates a huge works of their successor, I.C.I. Brunner Mond built a substantial village at the factory gates, with church and school, which still survives; well-built but not outstanding in architecture or layout. Winnington Hall, occupied and used by I.C.I., is of high quality — including work by one of the Wyatts on a 16th and 17th century house.

G5   **Winsford** has only two or three points of interest: Knight's Grange, originally a grange of Vale Royal Abbey, where there is now a restaurant; St. Chad's Church and its surroundings east of the Nantwich road; and England's only salt-mine, on the west bank of the Weaver. There is industrial archaeological interest on the old salt industry sites.

F1   **Winwick.** The prominent church with a tall spire contains some fine monuments (especially 15th — 17th centuries).

F8   **Wrenbury,** a pleasant enough village with a Perpendicular church, flanks the Llangollen Canal, with a wooden lift bridge like those painted by Van Gogh.

Bibliography and Acknowledgements

Books consulted and other articles include:

A History of Cheshire — J.J. Bagley, general editor (Cheshire Community Council)

Cheshire before the Romans — W.J. Varley — 1964
Roman Cheshire — F.H. Thompson — 1965
Pre-Conquest Cheshire, 383-1066 — J.D. Bu'lock — 1972
Cheshire under the Norman Earls — B.M.C. Husain — 1973
Cheshire under the Three Edwards — H.J. Hewitt — 1967
Cheshire in the Later Middle Ages — J.T. Driver — 1971
Tudor Cheshire — Joan Beck — 1969
The Civil Wars in Cheshire — R.N. Dore — 1966
Historical Atlas of Cheshire — Dorothy Sylvester & Geoffrey Nulty (Revised edition 1966)

A History of Widnes — G.E. Diggle — 1961
A History of Macclesfield — C. Stella Davies — 1961
A History of Congleton — Congleton Conservation Society
Social & Economic Development of Crewe — Chaloner, W.H. — 1950

Saltways from the Cheshire Wiches — W.B. Crump (In L.C.A.S. Vol 54, — 1939)
Salt in Cheshire — A.F. Calvert — 1914
A History of the Chemical Ind. in Widnes — D.W. Hardie — 1950
Lancashire Coal, Cheshire Salt and the Rise of Liverpool — T.C. Barker (In H.S.L.C. Vol 103, —1951)
The Chemical Revolution — A & N Clow — 1952
Navigations — North Wales & Cheshire Archaeological Society. Chester Archaeological Society

Sankey Canal, Trent & Mersey & Irwell Navigations — Bageley
Nicholson's Guide to the Waterways — North West — R. Nicholson

Railways of Britain — J. Simmons — 2nd edition — 1968
Railways in Cheshire, c. 1837 — 1939 — Historic Society of Lancs and Cheshire
Building of Railways in Cheshire down to 1860 — H.J. Hewitt — 1972
Cheshire Lines Railway — R.P. Griffiths — 1947

Communications and Transport in Medieval Cheshire — H.J. Hewitt (Chester Archaeological Society, NS Vol 27, — 1926-7)

Four Centuries of Cheshire Farming Systems — J.J. Bagley (Hist. Soc. of Lancs and Cheshire, Vol 106)

Cheshire — Its Cheese Makers — E. Driver — 1909

The Building of England — Cheshire — N. Pevsner & E. Hubbard — 1971
— S. Lancs — N. Pevsner — 1969

Lists of Buildings of Special Architectural or Historic Interest Schedules of Ancient Monuments — Department of the Environment

List & Map of Historic Monuments open to the public — 6th edition — 1972
Ancient Monuments in England — 6th edition — 1973
Ancient Monuments: Illustrated regional guides.

Two major works of 19th century scholarship are invaluable for general historical information on Cheshire (within its old boundaries), but make relatively little reference to the physical development of settlements and countryside.

History of the County Palatine and City of Chester — G. Ormerod, 2nd ed, 1882, Routledge

East Cheshire, Past & Present (2 vols) — J.P. Earwaker, 1880, Earwaker

A new Victoria History of Cheshire, which should be a most valuable addition to existing published sources, is shortly to be published.

The County Archivist and The Directors and staff of the County Libraries and Museums and Highways & Transportation Departments have given much valued help in the preparation of this review.

Index

The Gazetteer (Chapter 8) is not referred to in the Index.
Illustrations are in heavy type.

Illustrated by Vivienne Llewellin.
Design and Layout by Tony Meyers.